I0118138

Object to violence because when it appears to do good the good is only temporary the evil it does is permanent.

Mahatma Gandhi

Mogsdishu City Neighborhoods

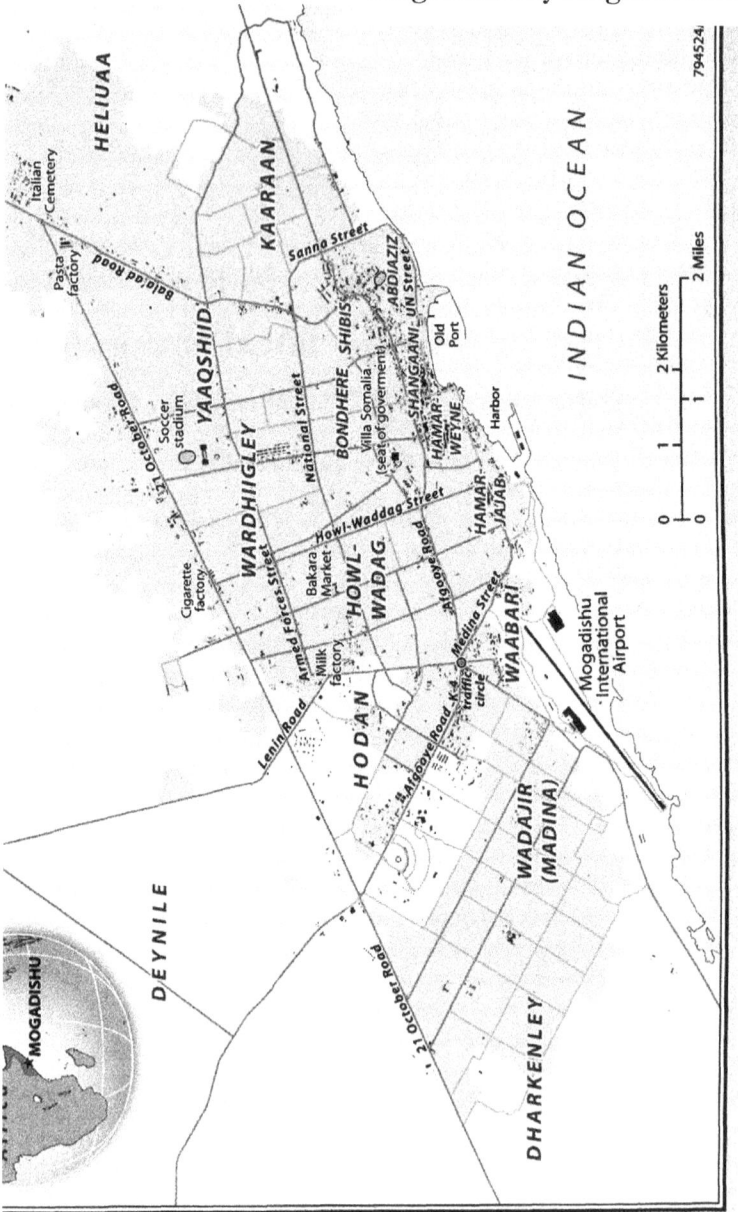

794524,

HELIUAA

KAARAAN

YAAQSHIID

WARDHIIGLEY

BONDHERE

SHIBIS

ABDIAZIZ

SHANGAANI

HAMAR-WEYNE

HAMAR-JAJAB

"HOWL"-WADAG

HODAN

WAABARI

WADAJIR (MADINA)

DEYNILE

DHARKENLEY

INDIAN OCEAN

Sanna Street

Italian Cemetery

Pasta factory

Balcad Road

21 October Road

Soccer stadium

National Street

Villa Somalia (seat of goverment)

UN Street

Old Port

Harbor

Howl-Waddag Street

Bakara Market

Cigarette factory

Armed Forces Street

Milk factory

Afgooye Road

Medina Street

Traffic circle

Afgooye Road

Lenin Road

21 October Road

Mogadishu International Airport

MOGADISHU

0   1   2 Kilometers

0   1   2 Miles

Out of Mogadishu

A memoir of the Somali Civil War in 1991

This is the story of the decline of Somali Nationalism, rise of 'calannism and missed opportunities to avert the Somali Civil War in January 1991.

Yusuf Mohamed Haid

Copyright@ 2016Yusuf Mohamed Haid
ISBN 10-0692610561

Reproducing, copying and transmitting
in any form of this book is prohibited.

Dedication

I humbly dedicate this book to the millions who lost their lives, disabled, or displaced in the Somali Civil War.

Acknowledgement

Many people helped me in writing this book. Its com-pletion could not have been possible without them and I gratefully acknowledge their contribution. In particular, I am deeply indebted to my family, Professor Lidwien E Kapteijns, Mr. Abdikarim Hassan of Wardheernews.com, and Mr. Abukar Hassan. I thank my relatives and friends who who provided me valuable support and advice during the writing of this book.

Content

Preface

On the morning of December 30, 1990, the residents of Mogadishu waked to a quiet, hot, and humid day. The children hurried to schools, and government employees flocked to their offices to help their relatives or/and those who could pay bribes. Businesses opened their doors, and the street vendors displayed their goods in open market stalls to attract shoppers. The bargain hunters milled about, jostling and shoving each other along the narrow lanes between the stalls and booths. The hi-fi speakers from teashops, shops, and the open market boomed the latest music. The tea shops served both hot and cold drinks and food to the perspiring stream of souls, including the tired and jobless, the criminals, the regime spies, and some who skipped work. At midday, most people retreated to their homes for lunch and siesta.

Then late in the afternoon, the United Somali Congress (USC) militia in the north of the city without warning fired the first shots of the Somali Civil War that destroyed the Somali state. Most people who yearned for an end to the suffocating rule of the oppressive regime welcomed the news. They were ready for any change that would free them from the hardship and repression that became a part of their life.

Unfortunately, a few days into the conflict, the warring parties, the USC militia, and regime security forces began to mobilize the civilian people against each other. As a result, hostility started among major clans, in particular, the Hawiye, Darod, and Isaq. The Hawiye clan was the majority in Mogadishu and the surrounding area, and it supported the USC militia and provided its fighters, supplies, and cover.

The warring parties also started decisive clan propaganda with hostility undertone. In the heat of the fighting, all tribes became susceptible to the hate propaganda. Soon after, most of the top brass of the government army, police, and militia left their posts and joined their clans, respectively. In a desperate move, the regime initiated a policy of 'divide and rule', and it gained support from some of the Darod clans who, until then, actively opposed the divisive tactic of the regime. These developments reinforced each other and altered the political dynamics in the country.

The president hanged on power even when partially the center of the city was destroyed. The USC movement failed to restrain its fighters, and it refused to coordinate its campaign with the rest of the opposition movements of SSDF, SNM, and SPM. It also allowed the marauding gangs to massacre innocent civilians, even the children belonging to the Darod and other sub-clans. The impacted clans include those who opposed the regime and suffered greatly under its oppression. Sadly, the conflict tossed the country into a crisis that was difficult to exit. As a result, the Somali nationalism began to wane, and Somali 'clannism' started to rise.

Regrettably, the regime, the opposition militias, and the International Community did not understand or care about the devastating consequence the conflict would have on the future of Somalia. It was perplexing why some actors, in particular, the International Community neglected the apparent opportunities to intervene boldly and dictate the outcome of the conflict.

This book was compiled from my journal entries, and it recounts what I saw or heard in Mogadishu during the first two weeks of the conflict. It also provides crucial insight into the Somali psyche at a time when the conflict was destroying the nation. The city lost its communication at the beginning of the conflict, and I was unable to verify the incidents I was hearing. Therefore, I apologize in case some of the events in the book do not reflect as they exactly occurred. The names of the people and places in the book are real, but in most cases, I used only the first or last name of the people. However, the names of the locations of the city are real. For those of you who did not live in Mogadishu city, I suggest referring the maps on the first and last pages of the book. I also encourage readers to acquire a basic knowledge of Somali history, culture, and genealogy.

I hope this book will shed light on the root causes of the 'Somali Clan War' (Somali Civil War). I believe the root cause of the conflict was the injustice and corruption of the regime, on the one hand, and the power-seeking leaders of the opposition movements. When I started writing this book, I was thinking of the people who were outside Mogadishu at the beginning of the conflict. I was also thinking of the people who were born after the year 1991. I hope the book would help these people understand the nature of the conflict, and it would also help them recognize the enormity of the conflict. Hopefully, it would explain the suffering and destruction the conflict caused the nation and how it devastated the lives of millions of people in numerous ways.

I believe the reconciliation of the Somali people requires a better understanding of what happened since the independence of 1960. I tried to be objective in recounting my experience of the conflict, its impact on Somali people, which is denied by some sections of the society. The conflict had been fermenting from the beginning of Somali Civilian Administrations of 1960 to 1969, into the Military Regime of 1969 to1991, and it was fueled by the clan-militias founded in Ethiopia after 1978. The Somali political strife caused unbelievable devastation in the period leading up to and following the events described in this memoir.

The book covers a specific period, just before the capital city was swept in the civil war violence, starting from December 26, 1990, to January 16, 1991. It was two weeks before the expulsion of the President Siad Bare from the city. The blame for the conflict entirely goes to two parties. First, the regime which failed to protect the civilian population and conducted a clan-based violence for years, and allowed the destruction of many communities. Secondly, the opposition militias which lacked agenda and patriotic vision. Perhaps the most serious blame goes to the leadership of the USC, SSDF, SNM and SPM militias whom the public held in a high standard, but orchestrated the Somali clans to kill each other. That was why my brother Abdi and his only son Hassan lost their life in the hands of the USC militia on January 14, 1991, simply because of their clan affiliation. In conclusion, in the long-run, the impact of the Somali Civil War and the clan-based violence of 1991 would be felt for generations to come.

December 31, 1990
Mogadishu, Somalia

The Coming of the Storm

On October 15, 1969, the state president Dr. Abdirashid Ali Shermaarke was assassinated in LasAnod town, and the prime minister Mohamed Haji Ibrahim Igal was on official visit outside the country. The national assembly was preparing to choose a new president, when army officers, on October 21, 1969, took over the government and the capital city and rounded up the senior government officials and other prominent politicians and sent them to jail. The coup leaders, led by the commander of the army Major General Mahammad Siad Barre quickly announced the formation of the Supreme Revolutionary Council (SRC), and declared war on tribalism, nepotism, corruption, and misrule and it renamed the country the Somali Democratic Republic. After almost 20 years in power, the Revolution was challenged by numerous clan-based militias and was ousted from power in January 1991.

Prior to the military takeover, two important events occurred in December 1990. The first was the fall of the town of Jowhar to the USC. The town is 91 km north of

Mogadishu, and its capture by the USC sparked concern in the capital city. Before the Jowhar incident, the Somali opposition groups operating from Ethiopia captured large areas throughout the country. It seemed the regime miscalculated the opposition capacity to score a significant victory and thought the Jowhar incident was a glitch in the security radar.

The Somali opposition movements (the USC, SSDF, SNM, and SPM)1, although established at different times, were all sup- ported by the Ethiopian Government. The Ethiopian leader, Mengistu Haile Mariam, who was humiliated by Somalia in the Ogaden War of 1977-1978, was bent on revenge. To achieve his goal, he armed and financed the Somali opposition movements and promoted their 'struggle' among Africa and socialist countries.

For the people in Mogadishu, the fall of Jowhar was a minor nuisance. They thought it was an isolated incident, and the army and other security forces would handle it. Little did they know how serious the event was, and that the capital itself would be on fire in a few days.

The second incident was personal. At the time, I was the man- aging director of Somali National Television, a department of the Somali Ministry of Information. On December 26, 1990, I arrived at the station at 7 am. I entered my office, and my secretary brought me the mail. I began checking the addresses on the envelopes, and suddenly a skinny envelope from the office of the Minister of Information drew my attention. After examining it for several minutes, I opened it. What a shock! The letter was a notification of my removal from the managing director position of the national television. It also instructed me to hand over the TV to the minister's cousin, a man named Kahin, who was the general director of Somali Broadcasting at the Ministry of Information. The tiny envelope containing just a few words brought an abrupt halt to my power and influence as the director of an important department of the Ministry of Information. In those days, it was a common occurrence to fire an officer from his or her position without justifiable reason.

The minister himself was newly appointed, and the new min- isters appoint their clan people to the important positions of their ministries. There was a public perception that the clans of ministers controlled the resource of their respective ministries. Although I was a presidential appointee, I was sure my minister had the approval of the President for my removal. I was sure the letter of my demotion from the office of President was on its way. Although the newly appointed director, Mr. Kahin, had been after the TV position for a long time, to some extent, I was responsible for my downfall. When I was ousted, I did not blame myself or the mistakes I had made. Instead, like most Somalis, I blamed others for my demise. I was unprepared for the sudden dishonor, and I began to act like an angry child. I handed the station to the new director on the morning of December 28.

In the afternoon, I decided to visit the minister. I went to his home, and he received me in his living room. The house was not furnished like the typical homes of ministers. It seemed he did not set up a 'milking' arrangement with the director of finance of the ministry. Without the unsanctioned arrangement with the finance department director, he was unable to convert his home into a luxury castle as all newly appointed ministers had done. He asked me to sit and then said, "Why have you come to see me?"

I said, "I would like to know why I am removed from my post." I knew he would not tell me why I demoted; nevertheless, I needed to unload my anger and frustration."

He began to enumerate the problems of the ministry and then detailed his plans to fix them. Finally, he looked at me and said, "I want to prop up the ministry. Thus, since Mr. Kahin has extensive experience in mass media, I want him to give the TV a new life."

"You are right!" I said sarcastically, "the whole country needs a new life, not only the television. However, what do you have for me?"

He hesitated for a moment and then got out of his chair and said, "I am thinking of a good position for you. Just be patient and wait a while." Then he looked at me and added, "I am sure you need a vacation after all those difficult years at the television!"

I also got out of the chair and said, "I know why you removed me, and it is not for the reasons you have stated."

He looked at me with surprise and said, "What do you mean?" Then, with mounting anger, frustration, and a bit of fear, I said, "You are a 'tribalist', and that is why you gave 'my job' to your cousin."

Without showing anger or resentment, he said, "If there is nothing else you want to say, you can leave now."

I left his house without a handshake and drove back to my home, boiling with anger. I believed none of what he said, and I was extremely bitter about losing my job.

I even wished hell for Somalia.

Then, on the afternoon of December 30, 1990, the USC militia brought the fighting deep into the north of the city. The following day, it began its attack on the government security forces in sev- eral locations, including the troops guarding the television station and surrounding areas. The explosion from the fighting echoed throughout the city, and panic struck the people. The loudspeak- ers of the mosques began to call the people to pray. Most of the people retreated to their homes before dark, and the streets were deserted. I was delighted! 'The regime is getting what it deserves,' I told myself.

At about 6:00 pm, the new television director came to my house and told me that the TV staff did not report for work. Usually, all the TV programs, except the news, were produced in the morning. The director asked me to help him locate the homes of the essential staff so the TV station could go on air for the 7:00 p.m. broadcast. We drove around the city in an attempt to assemble a skeleton staff of a technician, a camera operator, and an announcer. We visited the homes of the key TV staff, but all of them refused to go with us, and the broadcast time elapsed before we could put a team together. In the following morning, the station was looted, and its compound was littered with broken equip- ment, shredded tapes and documents, and damaged furniture. The USC militia used the heavy TV equipment, including the transmitter and antenna parts, monitors, and a broadcast van to block the main streets around the television area. The television station never came on air again. I laughed inside without thinking about the impact the conflict would have on the nation and me.

January 3, 1991
Mogadishu, Somalia

A Tale of Two Nights

It was the fifth night since the fighting between the United So-mali Congress militia (USC) and the Somali government erupted in Mogadishu. My area of the city was quiet; but I could hear the thud of explosions coming from the north of the city. The people in my area retreated to their homes at the sunset, and the streets were dead. The city lost even the intermittent electricity it was getting before the fighting broke out, and a dark blanket covered the city. The city also lost all communication the day the fighting started.

I was sitting alone in my living room, lighted with a dim, flickering, and smoking kerosene lamp. I had heard numerous stories about the events of the day, but I was not sure which or how many of them were true. However, it seemed the USC militia was creeping into the south of the city like a slow-moving flood. The demoralized government forces were barely in

control of the south of the city. It appeared the government was unable to put enough boots on the
ground to stop the advances of the highly motivated
USC fighters.

The readiness of the Somali army had been eroding
since the end of the Ogaden War of 1977-78. It did not
recover from the devastating defeat it suffered under the
combined socialist/communist forces led by the Soviet
Union. Besides, since the end of the Ogaden War, much
of its personnel deserted, and melted into the civilian
population or joined the various opposition groups
fighting the government. Furthermore, new recruits
were not joining the army for lack of resources and opportunities. Other national security organs such as the
police and the Revolutionary Vanguard Militia were also
ill-equipped and unable to carry out even their regular
duties. Those who stayed with the national army and
other security organs were waiting for an opportune
time to desert to save their skin.

Sitting in my semi-dark living room, I thought of
what the President was doing. I wondered what was
happening in Villa Somalia, where he lived and worked
that evening. I asked myself numerous questions, 'Is he,
as usual, sitting behind the drawer- less, sturdy table
under the tree, receiving the government officials and
guests alike? Or is he guiding the army commanders directing the forces fighting to the opposition militia at-
tempting to overrun the city? Are the waiting rooms and
the gardens of the compound crammed with visitors
waiting to see the president? Does the president have
time to receive the public tonight? Is the President, as
usual, chain-smoking and sipping a bitter black coffee,

washing its unpleasant taste with cold water? Is he re-laxed and in his inexpensive, casual clothes and sandals, or tense and in military fatigue?' I had no answers to these questions!

Like most African leaders, President Siad Barre ran the country by whim. He rarely signed any document ex-cept letters of pro- motion and demotion of civil and military personnel. He preferred to delegate the sign-ing of other papers to his ministers and senior govern-ment officials, after giving them thorough instructions. He kept all government affairs in his head, which was, I presume, the largest archive in the country.

I met the President several times. Some of my con-tacts with him were during my employment as the head of several govern- ment institutions. These institutions included Radio Mogadishu, the Somali Broadcasting Service (Radio Hargeisa and Mogadishu), and Somali National Television. In these meetings, I noticed that the life of the President was devoid of luxury. His offices had no expensive furniture or lavish decorations, and only a few revolutionary posters suspended on the walls. Many people who knew him attested to the fact that he did not stash riches in local or foreign banks. He did not build palace-like homes for himself or his family. His two wives continued to live in the government housing they had before he took the highest office in the country. The only plot of land he had in Mogadishu city, he do-nated to the Somali labor Organization, and it built its headquarter building on it. I believed that the only desire he had was to have an absolute power to control and dic-tate the life of the nation.

On the other hand, he was generous to those who

demonstrated loyalty to him. He appointed them to government jobs where they were able to amass absurd amounts of wealth in a very short time. He gave some of them the exclusive rights to import certain restricted goods, which they sold to the government institutions or to the public, and made a fortune in the   process.

In addition to my work-related encounters with the president, I had one extraordinary meeting with him, in which I got the opportunity to look closely into his personality and thinking. It was in 1980, when the presidential spokesperson, Mr. Abdi Haji Gobdon, told me that the President wanted me to join a committee 'working' in Villa Baydhaba. Later, I learned that the committee was writing the biography of the President. He also told me to continue to report to my regular jobs at the Ministry of Education's curriculum office and at Radio Mogadishu, and join the committee and work in the afternoons. He added that meals and a room to relax would be provided at the villa.

I was not sure why I was chosen, but at the time, I produced a weekly page for the only daily newspaper in the country, the Xiddigta Oktoober (October Star). I also produced a half-hour children program for Radio Mogadishu. Many people liked my style of writing, and I suspected that was the reason for my nomination to join the team writing Siad Barre's biography.

A few days later, I went to Villa Baydhaba. Professor Ali Jimale Ahmed and Professor Alinur Mohamed, who taught at Lafole Teacher Training College at the time, received me at the gate. Professor Ali Jimale was also a member of Mogadishu City Council and was rumored to be a close confidant of

the First Lady, Mama Khadija Moallim. Professor Alinur also worked part-time at Radio Mogadishu as an
English language newscaster. They were the team
writing the biography of the President. They took me
to the service quarters of the villa, where they
worked.

They briefed me about the project. They told me
about their visits to several parts of the country. In these
visits, they met many people who knew or were related
to the President. In those visits, they collected a large
amount of material, including stories, photos, and documents about the President. They interviewed many military and civilian officials, who knew or worked with the
president.

During our work at the Villa, we were allowed to use
the main building of the compound only one night. It
was the night we interviewed the Vice President, General Mohamed Ali Sa- mater, and one of the sons-in-law
of the president who was also the commander of the National Vanguard Militia. The commander, Abdirahman
Abdi Hussein (Abdirahman Guulwade), came with Mr.
Samater but did not interview him.

After we worked on the project for several more
months, we requested to interview the President before submitting the book for publication. Our request
was granted, and on the appointed day, we went to
Villa Somalia, the President's residence. The project
coordinator, Mr. Abdi Wayeel received us at the gate.
He led us to Villa Foresteria, the smallest villa of the
three villas in the compound. The other two bigger
villas were Villa Hargeisa and Villa Somalia. The attendants of the villa escorted us to a lightly furnished

corridor in the villa with several worn-out sofas and a coffee table. Through the end window of the corridor, we could see the President sitting in a dimly lighted spot beside the villa, and receiving people.

The villa had only a few rooms, and the walls of the corridor were bare. An old screen covered an open window facing the President, and it seemed it was shrouded with what looked like a spider web. We exchanged glances of surprise about the poor condition of the villa, and we contrasted it with the palace-like dwellings of government ministers and senior officials, which had orchards and an army of servants.

After a long wait, the President joined us. We sprang to our feet and stayed standing until he nodded for us to sit, and he dropped in a corner sofa. After he made several jokes, he turned serious, "I heard you are writing about my life! I assume by now you have found out everything about my past?"

Our lead man, Professor Ali Jimale spoke for us. "Comrade President, we thank you for entrusting upon us the writing of your biography. We also thank you very much for interrupting your busy schedule to meet us tonight. We need you to shed light on a few important questions we still have."

The presence of the President was overpowering, and Professor Ali's voice seemed to come from a hole in the ground. The quietness and the attention the President paid to Ali increased the tension in the room. Professor Ali continued his introduction with a tone full of fear and sometimes close to mumbling. He said, "We know that the life story of the Father of the Nation cannot be exhausted in a few months or years." He hesitated for a moment, "Even then, we are trying to record what we can for posterity. We would like you, comrade President, to tell us what you can from the long and fruitful struggle you led in shaping the destiny of our beloved country."

It was Friday, and the President was relaxed. He chain-smoked and continually took small sips from his coffee-cup. Suddenly, the first lady, Mama Khadija, showed-up and left after she quickly exchanged a few words and a joke with the President. The President's joke was about a Friday Somali family ritual1. There were no security people or aides in the room. Again, the President became serious and turned to Ali and asked, "What do you want to know?"

Ali fumbled for a moment, and then he went on to praise President lavishly. What he said could be summarized as, "We have already collected extensive information on your productive life and experience from your family members. We had also gathered important information from people you helped or guided, and from people who knew and admired you and whose lives crossed with you. Nonetheless, we would like to hear from you some aspects of your life. We need very much, your upbringing, your contribution to the decolonization struggle of our people. We would like to hear your revolutionary vision, and the future you are charting for our nation..."

The President interrupted Ali and began recounting his past. It seemed as though, for the first time, he was given a chance to add respectability to his past. He said, "My family was a nomad and in the 1920s lived in the Galgudud region. At the time, all adult male members of my family took part in the Dervish resistance against British, Italian, French, and Abyssinian colonizers. After the defeated the movement in the 1920s, some of my family members decided to move to Gedo region. They included the families of my father Siad Barre, alias Siad Garbaweyne[2], and his brother Farah Diliko. He paused for a moment and cleared his throat, "Unfortunately, on their way, shifta[3] killed my uncle, Farah Diliko in the Shilabo region. The rest of the family continued its journey to Gedo. Before the family arrived at its destination in Gedo, my father married Farah Diliko's widow Shaqlan Warfa, in accordance with Somali customs and Sharia. She conceived shortly, and I was born when the family arrived in　Gedo. I was named Mohamed."

Again, after a prolonged pause, he added, "At the age of ten, we heard the death of one of my uncles who stayed behind in Galgudud. My father left us to find out the circumstance of the death of his brother, and the condition of his family and other relatives in Galgudud. Later, we learned that my father joined Mr. Omar Samatar[4] militia fighting the Italian fascist army. He continued, "My father was fatally wounded in one of the encounters between Samatar militia and the Italian fascist army. The Samatar militia was overpowered, and it retreated carrying my wounded father."

He paused again and to light a cigarette. "My father died during the retreat, and they could not give him a proper burial." His voice became full of emotion. "They dropped my father in a bore- hole called Mareeg." He paused again, and his voice faded. "Days later, people in the area came to the borehole to draw water. They found a ballooned body blocking the mouth of the borehole.

They pulled him out and buried him properly."

He again paused and looked at us to check if we were listen- ing, and then he continued. "I was about fourteen when the news of my father's death reached us in Gedo. I decided to find out the events surrounding his death, and the livelihood of my other relatives in the Galgudud region. I left my mother with relatives, and I went to the city of Beledweyne in Hiran. I stayed at the home of a close relative Haji Masale. In Beledweyne, I learned more about the death of my father, and I also found more information about the rest of my family members. I continued to stay in Beledweyne until 1934 when I was recruited into the Italian Fascist army, which was preparing to invade Ethiopia. In Ethiopia, I came across diverse nationalities with different customs, cultures, languages, and history. I gained remarkable experience, which helped me later in life."

He continued recounting his experience in the early morning hours. He said, "... after Britain drove Italy out of Ethiopia, at the end of WWII, I joined the British East Africa army, which absorbed most of the Somali soldiers released by the Italian army. It was the time when all of the Somali inhabited territories in the Horn of Africa except Djibouti came under the control of the British Colonial Administration."

However, when in 1950, the UN placed Southern Somalia under Italian Trusteeship, he again joined the Italian Trusteeship Police, and he served in different departments, including the Criminal Investigation Department (CID).

On July 1st, 1960, when two portions of the five Somali inhabited territories5 got their independence from Italy and Great Britain, respectively. They united under the banner of the Somali Republic, and he joined the newly formed Somali National army. He was promoted in quick succession up to the rank of general, and he became the commander of the Somali armed forces within a short period. He held this position until October 1969, when he led a military coup that took power and ousted the legally elected government. Later, he promoted himself to the post of President of Somalia and Chair of the Somali Socialist Revolutionary Party, the only political party in the country.

It was three in the morning when he ended what he wanted to tell us, and then he asked us if we had questions. Professor Ali thanked him for sharing his 'extraordinary life with us, and then we asked him several questions. Since he worked for the Italian colonial administration for more than 20 years, we asked him if he recalls any of the Somali collaborators who betrayed the SYL liberation movement.

The question visibly surprised him, and he gave us a question- ing look, "Yes, I remember a number of them, and some of them are in my government." He paused for a moment, and then in a restrained voice; he added, "I cannot tell you who they are since I am the leader of all Somalis, the bad and the good. There is no perfect society in the world. A leader is the father of all citizens of a country and must protect all his/her people. A leader must protect even those who strayed from the right path at times and those forced by circumstance to make a wrong decision. Forgiveness is for all, as far as the law of the land allows." He took a draw from his cigarette and continued, "You know there is a Somali proverb which says, 'the head of a family and a midwife do not tell what they know.'"

We asked him in history the people he admired and the people he thought were great leaders. He named several but dwelled on the leader of the Dervish movement, Sayid Mohamed Abdulle Hasan. He said, "Sayid Mohamed was a great visionary who at- tempted to unite all Somali people under the Dervish movement and resist the advent of the European imperial powers." His words reminded us of Mark Antony's eulogy6 over the dead body of the assassinated Roman dictator Julius Caesar. He took time to light a cigarette and then continued, " Many Somalis do not know much about the achievements Sayid Mohamed Abdulle Hassan. They were taught only the Somali history written by foreigners. Said Mohamed Abdulle Hassan is the father of Somali nationalism and the founder of the Somali state."

We asked him why he regarded Sayid Mohamed as the founder of the Somali state. He smiled and said, "He is the founder of the Somali state because he defined the borders of Somali inhabited territories and created the Dervish army to defend it." He waited for his words to sink and then to prove the wisdom of Sayid Mohamed, and his accomplishment, he recited portions of several Sayid's poems, including the famous Dardaran7.

Marka hore dabku idinka dhigi, dumar Sidiisiiye,
Marka xiga dushuu idinka rare, sida dameeraha,
Marka xiga dalku idinku odhan,duunyo dhaafsada
e,

Marka xigana daabaqadda ayuu, idin dareensiine,
Dunjigeeda Soomaali dhan baa deyrka ka ahaaye,
Ragga Haatan igu diimayow, duxi ha kaa raacdo.

First, it will disarm you as though you are women folk,
Then it will load you as though you are donkeys,
Next, it will ask to exchange the land for pennies,
Finally, it will make you feel the poll-tax,
I was the protector of all Somalis,
You who are gloating at me, now,
 Enjoy what good it may do to you.

Close to the Morning Prayer, he rang a bell and got out of his chair. He thanked us for coming and for working on his biography. Instantly attendants rushed in, and they took us to our homes.

Months later, when we finished the writing, we drew interesting details from the past life of the President. He grew in an environment ravaged by drought, war, and famine, and faced numerous tragedies at a tender age, including the lost his father and uncles at difficult times. He participated in the Second World War and experienced a great deal of suffering, which affected his world outlook. Against all these odds, he was informed and possessed a thorough understanding of Somali politics, culture, and customs.

He had no formal education, but he spoke fluent English, Italian, Swahili, and good Arabic. He quoted verses from the poems of notable Somali poets whose words became part of Somali culture and literature, and he spiced his talk with proverbs and stories. He demonstrated remarkable intelligence and a sense of humor.

However, it seemed he was an idealist when it came to world affairs. His understanding of the prevailing global politics of the day was far from reality. He exaggerated the role that Somalia could play in world affairs, and he paralleled it with the super powers. He inflated the Somalia contribution and support to the liberation struggle of some of the African countries. He also treasured and held in high esteem the military culture and work ethics, and believed the only way to develop the undeveloped societies was giving them a military experience.

Tonight, after many years, I was sitting alone in my living room, lighted with a kerosene lamp. I wished I could see the President again. I thought of the man who dreamed of becoming the supreme leader of Great Somalia, fighting for the sovereignty of the only independent portion of the Somali inhabited territory. Whatever happens, I am sure he will have his place in Somali history.

January 4, 1991
Mogadishu, Somalia

A Message to Amina

What was happening in the north of the city was not clear. In the absence of mass media and telephones, the news circulated by word of mouth disseminated by the people fleeing the fighting on foot. It seemed that most of the population wanted the regime to be ousted, but they were not ready for the uncertainty accompanying the conflict.

In 1969, the army led by General Mohamed Siad Barre and other officers took power, and they called their action a revolution. Their vision of the future was apparent from how the coup was directed. The leaders of the coup and their advisors from the communist and socialist countries negated many aspects of the Somali culture, values, and beliefs. They introduced the ideology of scientific socialism with its economic and social dogmas and political system, all of which were incompatible with the Somali experience. Within a short time, the leaders of the coup established the Supreme Revolutionary Council (SRC), chaired by General Mohamed Siad Barre, and it transformed the socioeconomic system of the country.

The new revolutionary council asserted its power by militarizing the nation. The SRC first introduced military training for the government civil service, and after a few months, other sections of society were added to the training programs. First, diplomats and ministers of the overthrown regime were sent for training to Botico Military Camp in the suburb of Mogadishu city. After almost a year, the group was released, and another group of general directors of all government ministries and autonomous agencies followed them. It became the norm to send thousands of government employees, students, and civilians from all over the country to the military camps and district orientation centers for military training.

The 'military training' impacted certain sectors of society more than others. All secondary school graduates were sent for military training before they were allowed to apply for college, scholar- ship, or government jobs. A new subject called Cilmiga Bulshada (civics), which contained military doctrine, was added to the primary and secondary school curriculum. By 1975, the country was an oversized military camp.

When the Somali Revolutionary Socialist Party was inaugurated, it opened "Orientation Centers" in all large towns, districts, and villages of the country. The Centers taught the public on the basic principles of scientific socialism and conducted regular military training. They also spied on the government employees and the civilian population.

The process of preparing trainees was a humiliating

and night- marish experience. In 1972, I was among 800 male educators; the government called to Mogadishu from all over the country. The regime ordered us to take part in training at Botico Military Camp8. But first, we were instructed to undergo a medical screening at the military hospital in Mogadishu. Most of the educators were coming from out of Mogadishu, but they were not provided transportation. Some of us even did not know the location of the hospital, but most of us managed to find it on the appointed date. They kept us outside the hospital compound in the scorching sun before they allowed us in. Close to midday, they escorted us to the compound and then to a large hall in groups. Next, people in white gowns came into the hall and instructed us to form lines and undress. They told us to remove all our clothes, including our underwear. We were shocked since Islam and Somali culture, forbid exposing oneself publicly. Unfortunately, we did not dare to question them, and we undressed without objection to avoid being labeled antirevolutionaries.

The most important people in the education establishment – inspectors, headteachers, and teachers; senior administrators were in the group. The senior people who worked for decades for the Ministry of Education were standing naked in the queues. Shocked father-in-law and bother-in-law were in the same line and covered their private part with bare hands. They were embarrassed to look anywhere except the floor.

They instructed us to bend, and the people acting as hospital staff who were all male moved behind us and began to examine our bottoms. When they finished, they told us to report at Botico Military Camp the following day. We did not complain or talked about what happened. It seemed we went through one of the methods used to force people to submit and take orders without question. We wished we went through

The Botico military camp was at the edge of the Indian Ocean. We knew nothing about military regulation and rules, and we were scared but compelled to conform. The following morning, many of us reported at the camp as instructed. Low-ranking officers assembled us in an open area between rows of dormitory- like buildings, and we formed lines. We were bewildered and did not know what to expect next. The stillness of the place and the seriousness of the officers added to the terror we felt. After a roll- call, they took us to a warehouse and gave each of us a khaki short and a shirt, a blanket, and a military canteen bowl. Then they divided us into eight groups of about100 men each and took each group to one of the dormitory-like buildings.

My group was escorted to a hall containing rows of bunk beds. They assigned each person to a bed with a hard mattress, stuffed with dry grass, and covered with a piece of cloth. The old members of the group were given the bottom bunker beds, and the young men were assigned to the upper. The officers instructed us to change into the khaki shorts and shirts. But, before we could finish changing, we heard a shrill wind of whistles coming from the open area between the halls. The soldiers supervising us began to shout, "Hurry out to the assembly! Hurry out to the assembly!" They were wobbling their swagger sticks in the air as though they were directing frightened cattle. In a near panic, we rushed through the doors, pushing each other out of the way. In the open in front of the buildings, each group lined up separately and was given a company name. The low-ranking officers organizing us also lined up facing us in a military formation, from the lowest-ranking officers to the highest. Later, several senior officers joined them and lined up behind them.

Then, we noticed a highly decorated officer coming from the direction of the largest building in the camp. Some of us began murmuring his name – 'waa General Gabyow!' He was the 'commander' of the camp and head of the national civilian training program. As he came closer, one of the officers called us to attention and then turned and saluted him and gave him a report.

After the officer received a signal from the general, he turned to us and called us to ease. The general began to address us in a voice close to shouting. He said, "Welcome to the Botico Training Camp! From now until the day of your graduation, you will lead a strict military life. You will undergo physical and behavioral changes...." He continued in preaching voice for almost an hour, explaining the superiority of military life (work habit, discipline) over civilian life. As soon as he finished lecturing, the officers called us to attention and gave us marching orders. They led us to an open field at the edge of the Ocean, and the first drill of a six-month ordeal started for us.

The training was exhausting and tiresome. Every day, we were awakened at 4:30 am to perform personal tasks such as mak- ing bed washing and shaving. A running exercise of many Km outside the camp followed at 5 a.m. After we came back, we were assembled in the front yard of the barracks to exercise.

At about 6 a.m., we were given a break and a break-
fast of a piece of bread and tea. Again a 6:30 a.m., they
drove us back to the field at the edge of the ocean for
the morning drill. They stopped us at 12:30 p.m., and
we were given a small portion of spaghetti or rice
sprinkled with tomato sauce for lunch. At the end of
a 30-minute lunch break, they drove us back to the
field again for more drills, which continued until the
evening. At about 6 p.m., they served boiled beans
flavored with vegetable oil for dinner. After dinner,
they assembled us in a large hall for orientation ses-
sions given by un- educated drill instructors, who
talked about every 'imaginable' subject. They lectured
us on world politics and economic systems and the
basic concepts of scientific socialism. Every day, we
were dismissed at 8 p.m. to perform company duties,
including clean- ing the dormitories. We were allowed to lay down our tired backs at 8:30 p.m. We repeated the same routine every day at the same time.
The disabled teachers were exempted from exercises
and drills, but they were required to attend the orientation classes and to take part in the sanitation work
of the camp. After months of continues monotonous
daily running, drills, and orientations, many of the
trainees were drained and become sick, and some of
them hospitalized.

Camp life was terrible. There was no kitchen and
dining hall, and food was cooked in the open with bar-
rels. At mealtime, we queued in the open and received
our food in a canteen bowl. We ate in the open, sitting
on the dirt between the barracks. Within a few weeks,
we began to show discontent. However, it was for- bid-

den to complain against camp life or the regime. We knew that any show of grievance could be translated as a protest against the establishment and punishable with expulsion from the camp and termination from the government job.

Nonetheless, unexpectedly, a spontaneous protest poem began to emerge from the mealtime queues. Unknown individuals continued to add a line or couplet to the poem, and within a few weeks, the poem grew to many stanzas. At mealtime, more strings were added to the poem, and it became a long poem in a short time. The camp administrators found the poem and in- formed the Ministry of Education. The ministry sent a fact-find- ing team to meet us and if possible, to intimidate those who were suspected of coining the 'protest poem.'

Then one day after lunch, we were put in a hall instead of going to the field for drills to meet the team from the ministry of education. The team entered the hall, and after a quick introduction, it asked the poem and then told us that an antirevolutionary activity was not expected from the nation's educators. They also informed us to prepare for a teaching exam before our graduation from the training. We booed, and before the team finished their talk, we rushed out of the hall in protest.

It was in early 1972, and I believe it was the first time a group had dared to reject a program from an institution of the Revolution. Our action was extremely daring and dangerous. The revolution had imprisoned some of the country's former top leaders and even executed some of the coup leaders. The public was extremely fearful of the uncompromising actions of the regime. We later learned that the team reported what happened to the

Minister of Education, and in turn, the minister reported the incident to the office of the Supreme Revolutionary Council. We also heard that our action caused an out- rage, and the SRC instructed the Minister of Education to intervene and enforce the policies of the Revolution.

A few days later, a team led by the Minister of Edu- cation, Colonel Abdirazaq himself, came to the camp. The camp officials crammed us in a small hall, and un- easiness was generated the extreme heat and the pres- ence of the minster. After he talked with camp officials, he entered the hall, accompanied by a dozen men from the Ministry of Education and the camp officers. The min- ister and the camp commander, General Gabyow, sat behind a desk facing us, and the other men remained standing behind them. There were no loudspeakers, and the general began to ad- dress us in a deep voice, "Good morning! Today we are happy and honored to receive the Minister of Education, Colonel Abdirazaq, to talk about the future plans of ministry and the vision of our blessed Revolution." He faced the minister and contin- ued, "Comrade Minister, these are the teachers we are training, and we are happy with their collaboration and the maturity they exhibited. They are ready to hear your advice and   directives..."

The minster began to address us in a booming voice, but he was agitated and skipped the customary Islamic greeting. He began his talks by saying, "The other day, you showed disrespect to the officers from the Ministry that we sent here. We are not tolerating such behavior from the people the nation trusted to produce the leaders of tomorrow."

He looked at his notes for a moment and then continued, "The exam you were told the other day is for screening. We want to promote deserving teachers, and to send the rest to a teacher training school for more training."

At this point, we began to murmur and refuse to listen to him. He was annoyed, and his words became intimidating. He said, "We know some of you could not even write properly on the blackboard! Many teachers write from top to bottom on the board instead of left to right or right to left in case Arabic."

Someone from the back of the hall shouted, "You are right. Your wife must be one of the teachers who cannot write on the blackboard!" His wife was a teacher at one of the public schools. He rushed out of the hall without uttering another word.

On the following day, a commando unit from the town of Bal'ad replaced the regular camp trainers who were responsible for all our activities. The daily exercises, drills, and lectures turned into pure torture. We ran many miles outside the camp in the morning, and then came back and dug holes in the field and continuously filled up with rocks and then emptied them to be filled again. Our ordeal continued for many months without respite. In the process, teachers hurt and sent to health clinics in the camp or a hospital outside the camp.

Finally, many days, unexpectedly, one day before lunchtime, we were hastily hauled into a hall. We thought someone from the Ministry of Education or senior officer from the camp was coming to give us bad news. Instead, the chairman of SRC, Comrade Gen- eral Mohamed Siad Barre entered the hall. We were almost shocked, but we jumped on our feet in an army salute position. He scanned the hall, smiled, and after greeting signaled for us to relax and sit. He joked and laughed for a moment, and then turned serious and began addressing us without an introduction from the camp officials. After he spoke about the importance of the teaching job and its role in the nation-building, he posed and said, "I am here to hear your poem!"

We were surprised and looked at each other and could not say anything. He kept repeating the statement, but no one dared to answer. Then he looked at a man sitting in a corner and said, "Mr. Ali Jama, recite the poem for me!"

Mr. Ali Jama was a well-known poet and very much respected senior teacher from the north of the country. Ali did not deny or admit the existence of the poem. Instead, he said, "Comrade President, you mean the message the teachers sent to their wives back home?"

The president laughed and said, "Maybe! That is the poem. I want to hear it." Mr. Ali Jama recited the first few lines of the poem:

Ma ogtahay Aaminay Indian ooshinkaan agawareegaaye?
But ogtahay anfacadaan cunaa Ma laha iidaane?
Ma ogtahay Askari jaahilaan amar ka qaataaye?
Ma ogtahay waxaan eersadaa odayga weeyaane?

Do you know Amina, I wander by the Indian Ocean?
Do you know the food I eat has no flavor?
Do you know I take orders from illiterate corporal?
Do you know I blame the older man for my ordeals?

The president interrupted Ali, and asked him, "Who is the old man (odayga) you are blaming for your ordeal?"

Mr. Ali paused for a moment, and then said without vigor, "Comrade President, the poem is a collection, and every line be- longs to someone in the group. I do not know who added that line. However, I believe whoever added the line was thinking of the Minister of Education."

The president laughed and left after a few more comments and jocks. Instantly, all the training activities were relaxed, and the trainers of the camp again replaced commandos that were brought from Bal'ad town. The Ministry also canceled the exam it planned to give. I believe the poem, which had hundreds of stanzas, was one of the first protest poems against the October Revolution of 1969.

After torture like six-month training, we took part in the yearly celebration of the Revolution parade held on October 21, 1972, at the July 1st Square in Mogadishu. We graduated from the train- ing the following day and were set free to join civilian life again. Most of us were brainwashed and believed in the absolute truth of the principles of scientific socialism. We began to accept what- ever the government threw at the public to be the truth. We thought in socialism, the state provides each member of the society 'what he/she needs'.

The socialist indoctrination and the acceleration of military training greatly impacted the public, and it seemed they believed that there was nothing that they cannot overcome. The Revolution leaders suspended the constitution and customary laws, and circulars and proclamations ran the state. The office of the SRC, chaired by General Mohamed Siad Barre, issued all revolutionary proclamations and directives.

The public took part in the militarization and orientation pro- grams conducted at the orientation centers, government institutions, and military camps all over the country. The people followed the government directives without question and finally began to enjoy the military culture, which became fashionable. The Military jargon became a part of the mainstream lexicon. Thousands of people attended, and many others followed on the radio and television the military parades, which were very much admired by the public. The spectators of the military parades praised the height of the lifted knee, especially when it gets close to the chin. The military uniform became a fashion, and govern- ment employees and businessmen tailored their clothes in the safari-style of the military uniform. The mass media, which was controlled by the government, entertained the public mainly with revolutionary songs and martial music.

The public began to believe the state propaganda conducted by the mass media and Orientation Centers. Most people thought socialism was the only path to the future prosperity of the country. It was a standard requirement to hang on the walls of government offices the quotations and pictures of socialist/communist thinkers. They were also displayed on the wall and streets of towns and cities all over the country. Many People memorized quotations of Karl Marx9, Lenin, and other socialist and communist philosophers. The memorization of the quotations became the measuring stick of a person's education level, and how conversant one was in the principles of socialism and communism. It was common to meet someone who could re- cite socialist and communist quotations. Some of the quotes were very popular. The famous quotations included, "Let the ruling classes tremble at a communist revolution. The proletarians have nothing to lose but their chains. They have a world to win, and

Working men of all countries, unite!' When the destitute people heard such a flowery call, they often believed and blindly followed the messages of the Revolution.

The regime allocated most of the state resources to the military buildup. As a result, the Somali army became one of the strongest in Africa. The Revolutionary government also began biting the drums of nationalism, war, and the obligation to liberate the So- mali brothers under the colonial rule of Ethiopia and Kenya. The militarization and the rise of Somali nationalism grew hand-in- hand, and the call to free the 'missing' portions of the 'Somali Nation' grew louder by the day. The liberation pitch reached its height in 1976 when the Revolutionary government began to pre- pare the nation for war in public in speeches, songs, poems, and plays. The revolutionary calls were continuously spread by the mass media owned by the government, and the people became ready to liberate their 'brothers and sisters' under the yoke of colonialism, namely the two Somali inhabited territories occupied by Ethiopia and Kenya, respectively.

In 1976, the Somali Revolutionary Council issued a significant decree which promoted general Mohamed Siad Barre to the post of the President of the Somali Socialist Democratic Republic (SSDR). This was in addition to the previous positions he held of the Chair of the SRC and the Chair of the Socialist Revolutionary Socialist Party (SRSP), the only political party in the country. The word of the President became the law of the land. All government institutions disregarded the practice of planning, proper manage- ment, and reporting proce- dures and just followed the daily directives of the presi- dent, which was published on October Star Newspaper and broadcasted on radio. It was a culture adopted from the North Korea dictator comrade Kim Il Sung.

Most of the Somali poets, playwrights, composers, and other artists produced a cascade of songs, dramas, poems, and posters and other material praising the 'Blessed Revolution and its leader.' They coined many titles for the President, which included the Father of the Nation, the Guiding Light, the Saver, the Torch Bearer, and the Lion of Africa.

By the end of 1976, the adulation and admiration in- toxicated the president, and he began to depend less and less on the advice of the socialist and communist coun- tries. These nations gave So- malia continuous assistance and military equipment and training since the birth of the October Revolution in 1969. The support was mainly to promote the Somali socialist economy and political system. The Somali Government even established eco- nomic ties with the dreaded regime of North Korea. The Somali regime awarded contracts to the cash-strapped North Korean Govern- ment to build several statues, in- cluding those of Sayid Mohamed Abdulle Hassan, Stone thrower, Hawo Tako, and Ahmed Gurey. The Somali Revolution adopted the North Korea propaganda- style by decorating the cities and towns of the country with hundreds of posters. The posters showed the president raising his right hand, pointing to images of factories, fields of farming, schools, and many other images alike Comrade Kim with the captions of 'the prosperity of tomorrow.'

The public enthusiasm for actualizing the dream of 'Great So- malia' and the boldness of the President reached its peak in 1976 when Somalia supported the struggle of Western Somali Liberation Front (WSLF) gorilla actions in Ethiopia. Units from the So- mali army in civilian clothes joined the front militias. After prolonged skirmishes, the hostility turned into a full-fledged war of the Ogaden War of 19977-78 between Somalia and Ethiopia. In the beginning, WSLF and Somali army captured most of the Western Somali territory in Ethiopia. However, they were booted out by the combined forces of socialist and communist countries led by Cuba and the Soviet Union. According to reliable sources, the Soviet Union urged Ethiopia not to invade Somalia.

Even though It heeded to the Soviet Union's advice, but the Ethiopian ambition to push its border to the coast of the Indian Ocean remained the same. It just waits for an opportune time to carry out its age-old pursuit of the Ethiopian kings. The Ethiopian design to incorporate its neighboring nations into its territory could be traced as far back as 1897. Emperor Menelik[10] of Ethiopia declared in a letter to the leaders of France, Germany, Italy, and Russia, his intention to capture many eastern and central Africa nations. The letter of Menelik II to the European kings stated, "While tracing today the actual boundaries of my Empire, I shall endeavor, if God gives me life and strength, to re-establish the ancient frontiers (tributaries) of Ethiopia up to Khartoum, and as Lake Nyanza with all the Gallas. Ethiopia has been for fourteen centuries a Christian island in a sea of pagans. If powers (Euro-pean) at a distance come forward to partition Africa between them, I do not intend to be an indifferent spectator.

As the Almighty has protected Ethiopia up to this day, I have confidence. He will continue to protect her and increase her borders in the future. I am certain He will not suffer her to be divided among other Powers.

Formerly the boundary of Ethiopia was the sea. Having lacked strength sufficient, and having received no help from Christian Powers, our frontier on the seacoast fell into the power of the Muslim-man. At present, we do not intend to regain our sea frontier by force, but we trust that the Christian Power, guided by our Savior, will restore to us our sea-coast line, at any rate, certain points on the coast."

Addis Ababa, 4th May 1897. Since the reign of Menelik II, Ethiopia's never abandoned the dream of annexing the nations of Horn of Africa.

Throughout the Ogaden War, both the Soviet Union and the USA abandoned Somalia. The Somali regime led by president Said Bare felt both the internal and external threats. To counter the threats, the Somali Revolutionary Socialist Party organized massive demonstrations in Mogadishu and throughout the country to support the president and the regime and to bust public and military morale. During one of these demonstrations, thou- sands of people assembled at the Sayid Mohamed Abdulle Has- san Square, next to the National Hall in Mogadishu. The Ministry of Information and National Guidance an organ of the party in- stalled a public address system with very powerful loudspeakers at the square and the surrounding areas. The president arrived and delivered an impassioned speech, concluding with the words, "We say to the Soviet Union cazzo!11 We say to the USA cazzo! We do not need their help! We will liberate our people and land." In the following months, the president became unpredictable and made many hasty decisions that set the country on a path of self-destruction.

In 1978, the defeated and demoralized Somali army lost most of its personnel and equipment. The senior officers were not happy with the way the war conducted and its outcome. As a result, in April 1978, a group of disgruntled army officers organized a coup but failed. Several of the officers were arrested and ac- cused of being the ringleaders. It was a hasty exe- cution without a proper trial. Most of the slain offi- cers were from the Majeerteen clan.

Following the swift execution of the officers, many Majerteen officers, including the founder of the SSDF, Colonel Abdillahi Yusuf, fled to Ethiopia. The Ethiopian government received them with great interest and helped them establish the SSDF opposition movement. It was the first Somali opposition movement formed in Ethiopia, a traditional enemy of Somalia. The news of the formation of the Somali opposition group of SSDF in Ethiopia spread quickly. An exodus of Somali politicians and military of- ficers fled to Ethiopia from major clans, who were not content with the Somali regime. They cre- ated more clan-based opposition movements operating from Ethiopia against the Somali regime. The Isaq clan formed the Somali National Movement (SNM), the

Hawiye inaugurated the United Somali Congress (USC), and later the Ogaden clan formed the Somali Patriotic Movement (SPM). As a result, these opposition movements put the final nail in the coffin of the age-old dream of 'Great Somalia.'

The clan-based opposition movements quickly established armed militias. They commenced a guerrilla war against the So- mali state and against specific Somali clans whom they suspected rightly or wrongly to be regime supporters. The militias quickly scored notable victories, and as a result, many individuals from the Somali army forces and civil service joined the opposition groups in Ethiopia. Most of the defectors were from the disgruntled clans that believed they were excluded from political participation and economic opportunities. In response to the danger posed by the opposition movements, the regime collectively punished members of the opposing clans. It also purged many members of these clans from the armed forces and civil service. The number of clans that were loyal to the regime began to shrink. Only the tribe of the president of Marehan and a few others remained faithful to the government. Consequently, the Somali clan infighting increased, and the decline of Somali nationalism accelerated. Above all, into motion was set the rise of Somali clan politics.

January 5, 1991
Mogadishu, Somalia

Batulo Goes Home

The rumble of fighting came closer to where I lived on the south side of the city. According to the rumors I was hearing, the USC militia had the upper hand in most of the encounters with the regime forces. It seemed the government soldiers had no de- sire to fight, and the government had no incentive to moti- vate them or justify the fighting against the USC mili- tia. The stress of the conflict and the clan-based political mobilization that accompanied, induced much fear and uncertainty in most people.

Late in the evening, I was sitting in my living room when I heard a sobbing coming from another room of my apartment. I quickly went there to find out what was happening. My mother, my wife, and my sister were crouching over Batulo, our maid of many years. When I asked them what happened, my wife looked at me, with tears in her eyes, and said, "Batulo is leaving us!" I asked them why she was leaving. None of them answered. I turned to Batulo and asked her why she was leaving.

In a low and trembling voice, she said, "My parents want me to join them."

Batulo was 20 years old, and she had been with us since she was only sixteen years old. She became a member of our family, and my children loved her very much. Her parents were farmers and lived in a farming village about eight kilometers east of Afgoe town. They visited us often and brought us produce when- ever they came to see their daughter and us. Usually, they stayed with us a few days at a time to reassure Batulo and to collect her salary. I tried to persuade her not to go, and I explained to her the danger she would face on the road. However, she insisted on leaving in the morning with other people from her village. I understood her concern. It became a part of the Somali experience to feel safe only among ones kin. It was a perception created by the age-old conflicts among Somali tribes.

For many years, the Somali tribes, in particular, the nomads, raided each other on meager resources of water and grazing land. These frequent, unpredictable, and destructive conflicts created a deep-seated hostility, suspicion, and state of vigilance among them. Moreover, the arrival of the European colonial powers in Somalia in the 18th century and their policies of divide and rule negatively impacted the already poor communal relations. The Somali tribes were unable to defend their common interests against invading enemy powers.

Although the Somali people were aware of the 'grand-design' of the colonial powers, and in many instances, waged isolated resistance wars against them (in particular, the British, the Italians, and Abyssinian), they were outmaneuvered, outgunned, and their land was partitioned into five parts. Furthermore, the colo- nial powers succeeded in driving wedges between the Somali tribes to prevent their unity. The colonizers were able to inject fear and mistrust among them, which still today continues to linger and cause turmoil even after some parts of Somali   territories gained independence in 1960.

Early in the conflict, I had several conversations with my old brother, Abdi Mohamed, who respected and ad-mired his knowledge of Somali history and culture. One day, we were talking about the fighting when suddenly he lamented, "History repeats itself! Our people have suffered enough already!"

I asked him what he was thinking and what he can tell me about the past Somali conflicts. He began to nar-rate how tribalism plagued the Somali people since the 15th century and beyond. He said, "Do you know that the hero and Islamist Ahmed Gurey campaigned to stop the Abyssinian expansion into Somali inhabited territo-ries? Sadly, The European colonizers and feudal Euro-pean Christian kingdoms supported Abyssinia, and it captured a large portion of the territory." He continued, " The Ahmed Gurey campaign ended after he was mur-der by a Portuguese sniper in 1543. His mighty army dis-persed into their clans and retreated to their respective areas, looting communities in their path."

I politely questioned his argument, "I thought Ahmed Gurey movement was a part of the Crusade Wars between Muslims and Christian Europe for the control of the holy city of Jerusalem. I believe he was a part of the Ottoman Empire army, which led the Muslim campaign against the Christian invasion and defeated with the rest of the Muslim army?"

Then I asked him," Was he resisting colonial intent into Somali territory?"

Abdi partially agreed but added, "It is true that he was a part of the Jihad campaign (crusade) defending the holy city of Jerusalem against European crusaders. However, his army came from various Somali tribes, and that resulted in disunity and cohesion in his army. He resisted the Abyssinian expansion into Somaliland." Then he added, " Again, the great Somali hero Sayid Mohamed Abdulle Hassan raised a mighty army of Dervishes from the Somali tribes to resist the invading European colonizers. He was able to unite many Somali clans in the name of the Somali nation, but in the end, tribalism set in, and the Dervish movement was defeated."

I said to him, "But many historians believe that the Dervish movement was defeated because it abandoned its guerrilla war when It established permanent settlements such as Taleh and others, which limited its guerrilla tactics of hit and ran."

He rebuffed, "Well, there are others who blame the attack of those settlements by Britain, which was the first aerial bombard- ment in Africa." He continued, "Again, that is not my point. I am trying to explain how tribalism has always dismantled the unity of Somali people." He added, "After the end of the Dervish move- ment, the Somali youth came together and founded the SYL organization in 1943. After a long and hard struggle, the SYL achieved its goal in 1960. The SYL party delivered the independence of two parts of the Somali inhabited territories from British and Italian colonizers." After a long pause, he added, "Unfortunately, in 1969 the Somali people forgot the independence struggle and sacrifices of the past generations, and awakened from slumber their worst enemy, tribalism. They established more than 84 clan-based political parties, and chaos, insecurity, and tribal infight ensued and pushed the country into a brink of disintegration. That is why the army intervened and took power in 1969 to save the nation." He continued, "The army seizure of power was to prevent the fragmentation of the country. Today, after the army in the name of the revolution kept hostage the aspirations of the people for more than twenty years, it lost legitimacy and grip on the power. The army itself was riddled with tribalism since it took the seat of the government. When the conflict started, we were witnessing the end of the era of tribal strife for political power and control of the meager national resources."

I was overwhelmed by the accounts of the Somali experience and the uncertain future facing them. I was afraid the Mogadishu conflict would hurl the country into a vicious cycle of never-end- ing clan infighting and self-destruction. I said to my brother, "The present polarization of the Somali clans along tribal lines may ignite a 'civil war,' and I hope Somali wisdom that 'in a war, a boy dies; and a boy is not born' will prevail. The regime, the opposition, and the political groups, including the Manifesto Commit- tee, will save the country destruction and would be able to restore the peace."

My brother showed little hope that the warring sides would restore peace, and he murmured, "Let us hope the best for our children!"

The unifying Somali voices of Ahmed Gurey, Sayid Mohamed Abulle Hassan, SYL, and many other movements such as the Biyamal movement in the south of the country, called on the So- mali people to unite and protect their land and way of life. Whenever the Somali tribal infighting becomes too destructive and violent, these voices urged the Somali people to look into their shared experiences instead of magnifying their differences.

For instance, the Dervish movement leader, Sayid Mohamed Abdulle Hassan, called on all Somalis 'to take arms and fight the colonizers who were bent to enslave them.' He employed compelling poems and founded the Somali dervish movement and fought the colonizers who came from afar to take their land. He assembled a powerful army and convinced all Somalis to defend their culture, religion, and nation.

Similarly, more than 20 years later, after the death of Sayid Mohamed, the unifying voice of the SYL was heard in all corners of the land. The SYL campaigned endeavored to stop Somali clan infighting, and it crusaded for the Somali unity and independence. The rallying cry of League (SYL) was:

"Oh, Somalis wake up,
Wake up and lean on each other,
and always support the weakest among you!"

After Somalia gained independence, the Somali leaders be- tween 1960 and 1969 could not establish a working democracy. The Somali nationalist vision of SYL that delivered the Somali in- dependence and the Somali Re-

public in 1960 waned after corruption and clannish became rampant in the country. Manifold clan-based political parties were formed to take part in the 1969 national
election. Mr. Abdirashid Ali Sharmarke, the state president, was also assassinated in the town of Lasanod in Sol
region. In light of this competition and political infighting among the newly formed political parties, it was ev-
ident that the country was sliding into a civil war.

To avert the imminent danger the country was facing, the national army, which was the only organized
force in the country, staged a coup on October 21, 1969,
and hijacked the government. The coup prevented the
republic from disintegrating into clan- controlled enclaves. In their first communique, the coup leaders declared that they took power, 'to save the country from
tribal- ism.' They immediately introduced anti-tribalism
directives and programs and disseminated them over the
government-con- trolled mass media. One of the famous
slogans they coined to fight tribalism was: 'Tell us what
you know, do not tell us whom you know....'

Unfortunately, the deep-seated Somali conviction
of the 'US and THEM' persisted and manifested itself
in different shades in society. But, the leaders of the
coup were determined to purge all facets of tribalism
from the public discourse. They declared the equality
of all Somalis under the law. They highlighted the destructive nature of tribalism and its lasting negative
impact on the unity and progress of the nation. Above
all, they proclaimed laws that prohibit tribalism in all
its manifestation.

A few months later, and after the coup transformed
itself into a Revolution led by the SRC, its leaders de-

greed to entomb tribalism permanently. After an extensive campaign of exposing the negative aspects of tribalism and its reactionary nature, a date was set for its
symbolic burial. On the day set for the burial, people
gathered in groups in public places in cities, towns, and
villages all over the country. They built ugly and mon-
strous effigies, symbolizing the face of tribalism, dug
graves, and in a euphoric and celebratory atmosphere
buried the effigies.

However, many people were skeptical of government campaigns and intensions. Nevertheless, they performed what the regime wanted, and most of them were
'following the tide' to evade the anti-revolutionary label.
I recall a friend of mine who told me what they did on
the burial day. He was a teacher at HamarJajab middle
school, located on the edge of the Indian Ocean. He said
sarcastically, "Sorry! We dug a deep pit in the ground,
and we placed tribalism at the bottom of the pit. Unfortunately, it jumped out and jumped into the ocean. It escaped from us!" He added, "But it was badly wounded,
and it will not swim far, and it will not survive along!"

The question remained why tribalism persists in
Somali life and why it causes havoc every ten years or
so, and why people trust their clans more than the
state? The answers to these   questions are compli-
cated, but it seems ordinary people feel safe under
their clan protection, and they did not see much good
in most of the national leaders.

When the conflict broke out in Mogadishu at the
end of 1990, some of the people who wanted to leave
the city usually stayed because they did not know
where to go. Many of them, their clan areas were in

remote parts of the country, and the presumed 'enemy clans' or unruly militias controlled the roads. The lack of transportation was another serious problem that deterred people from exposing themselves to the invisible dangers. Also, many of them never visited their tribe areas and were strangers to their kin. The dilemma they faced was 'to stay where they were perhaps to be killed or like Batulo, try to reach their clan area and risk the possibility of dying on the road.

When the conflict broke out in Mogadishu at the end of 1990, some of the people who wanted to leave the city usually stayed because they did not know where to go. Many of them, their clan areas were in remote parts of the country, and the presumed 'enemy clans' or unruly militias controlled the roads. The lack of transportation was another serious problem that deterred people from exposing themselves to the invisible dangers. Also, many of them never visited their tribe's area and were strangers to their kin. The dilemma they faced was 'to stay where they were perhaps to be killed or like Batulo, try to reach their clan area and risk dying on the road.

The life of the ordinary people in the city of Mogadishu be- came unbearable as the conflict deepened. Uncertainty settled in, the fear of the unknown became real, and people did not know where to go for protection. I understood why my maid Batulo was fearful and wanted to join her family and clan near Afgoe. She was determined to reach her kin in the face of menacing danger on her way.

People didn't trust their neighbors anymore, and the peaceful days when neighbors visited each other and socialized were pushed to memory. The children stopped playing in the streets and neighborhood yards, and their laughter that swelled the air disappeared. The sight of the groups of people strolling in streets, dressed in colorful clothes, vanished. The occasions that brought thousands of enthusiast spectators who jammed the stadiums, and roared and clapped in support of their teams were gone. Forgotten were the good old days when the Somali people traveled from one part of the country to another without carrying food or money, and the communities in their path fed them. Gone were the gatherings in public spaces on holidays such as the Eid and praying and wishing each other peace, prosperity, and happiness. For most people, the future was dark, and they wished the conflict to vanish as morning dew and peace restored. Sadly, some of the present Somali leaders are still wailing like the leaders of the 84 parties of 1969, which brought the blessed October Revolution to save the county.

January 6, 1991
Mogadishu, Somalia

Clan Polarization

The regime hardliners who were concerned about their 'state welfare' and the unscrupulous leaders of the Hawiye and Isaq militias of USC and SNM, and other anti-government groups succeeded in turning the conflict into a fight between Hawiye and Isaq and Darod. The daily exodus of the displaced people arriving from the combat areas of the north to the south side of the city continued and increased. They came with small bundles of possessions and children on their backs. They reported the intensification of the fighting, and the USC efforts to secure a victory before Hawiye public support fades. I heard the Hawiye traditional leaders, politicians, and intellectuals who regularly met at the Lafaweyn Hotel announced their support to the USC fight and called on the regime to surrender power.

Unfortunately, both sides of the conflict, the regime, and the opposition militias miscalculated the consequence of the conflict. The USC assumed it had public support, and believed it would score a quick victory if it forces out the President and what remained of his forces and supporters out of Mogadishu. However, in reality, the regime had substantial support from some Darod clans, from even some Hawiye tribes and other minority Somali clans. However, the regime miscalculated the strength of the op- position and thought USC was a pack of a ragtag group that was interested only in looting the city and raping women. The regime also believed that since the USC movement lacked combat experience, effective organization, and was led by inexperienced individuals, it would fade away within a few weeks. However, days into the fighting, both sides realized that their calculations were off the mark. In reality, USC had diverse support that included Hawiye clans, and several non-Hawiye clans, including sympathizers in SPM and the SSDF militias. Besides, the USC proved to be a formidable force with sophisticated urban fighting tactics and had a well-established central command. A week passed, and the regime realized that it would be impossible to win the war, as long as the USC enjoys the support of Hawiye clans, and fights on its turf.

The USC militia revised its strategy to quicken the downfall of the regime. It assigned each Hawiye sub-clan to an area of the city to liberate or defend. The regime quickly responded to the USC move by redeploying its forces and stationing them in strategic locations to counter the USC new strategy. Both sides started a dangerous and divisive campaign among their supporters by spreading rumors that 'their enemy' was conspiring to annihilate them. A rumor circulated that the USC leaders were bent on over- throwing what they called the 'Darod regime', and was aiming at driving all the Darod people out of Mogadishu. On the other hand, some Darod clans deceived by the regime propaganda began to organize their defenses. Unfortunately, only the tribes which had militias that were founded, supported, equipped, and financed by Ethiopia, were able to fight forcefully and challenge the regime and its supporters.

After USC decided and focused on the Darod expulsion, prominent Hawiye and Darod politicians and businesspeople began to organize and equip their respective tribes. They were the individuals who had a lot to lose if their side did not win the fight. They began mobilizing their clans and forge alliances with other groups that were not the main rivals in the conflict and sympathetic to their cause. Each side collected supplies recruited fighters and sent them to the defense lines. They even persuaded the downtrodden youth who had never tasted

the bounty of their nation to join the fight and defend the 'clan honor.' In respective clan meetings, sponsoring politicians and businesspeople on both sides emphasized 'the past glory of their clan, its good name, and its reputable standing in Somali society.' They then reminded their audiences of the need to defend the past glory of the clan and prevent angering the spirit of their dead ancestries. Both warring sides continuously held regular meetings and gave inflammatory speeches, distributed arms to the participants, and dispatched them to join or relief the men at critical locations throughout the city.

The bombardment of the hate propaganda from all sides of the fight confused and frightened the ordinary people, and they were unable to reach informed decisions. The people missed the fact that the conflict was a power struggle between the militia leaders who could not win the power lawfully and in a democratic process,

and the sitting President and regime that lacked legitimacy and refused to yield the power. Many people accepted the clan hate propaganda and joined the fight.

Despite the spreading insecurity in the city, some
people did not realize the seriousness of the situation.
Many of them were absorbed by the decades of regime
propaganda, which they in- ternalized, and unable to
grasp the danger they were facing. They believed the situation was under government control, and the regime
reinforced their assumption by continually spewing
propaganda through its mass media outlets. It continued
preaching the power of the 'Blessed Revolution,' the glorious destiny of the nation, and its ultimate victory over
its enemies. Many people doubted the promise of the
Revolution and wished one of the warring sides to win
and restore the peace.

Sadly, for some clans, the reality came quickly. They
were hunted and executed by other tribes just for being
a minority, or just for being from the 'enemy' or a hostile
clan. For some people, persecution was simply because
of their clan affiliation, and they did not have the luxury
to wait the government to restore peace. My wife was
one of those people who envisioned a clan-based assault
and expulsion. She took our three boys and joined my
in- laws traveling to Kismayo, in the south of the country. My paralyzed mother, my sister, and two of my
brothers and a nephew stayed behind. Many other families loaded what they could on cars, trucks, and even on
carts and left the city. There was no electricity since the
start of the conflict, and a dark blanket covered the city
at night. The artillery reverberation coming from the
frontline, and the stench of the gunpowder in the

air compounded the dread the people felt.

My oldest brother Abdi was a typical mosque goer, and after the morning prayer, he usually went to meeting places in the city to find the news of the day. I met him at the neighborhood mosque for the midday prayer. We left the mosque together after we prayed, and on our way home, I asked him the talk of the day and the situation of the fighting.

He said, "The people are saying the USC militia is ready to launch a final assault on Villa Somalia and other important locations held by the regime forces." He added, "Hopefully, that will bring the conflict to an end." After a long pause, he continued, "Some people are saying every Hawiye sub clan is given a front to liberate or defend. They assigned the Abgal clan to 'liberate' Bondhere and Wardhiglay districts and the neighborhoods around Sinai market. The Habargidir clan is assigned to engage the 'enemy' in the livestock market, Lido and Kambo Amharo neighborhoods, and to lead the attack on all government positions, including Villa Somalia. The remaining Hawiye clans were assigned to defend the 'liberated' areas, manage and deliver supplies, and cover the needs of the 'frontline' operations." These responsibilities of Hawiye clans later turned into USC planning and policy committees. In addition to the given objectives, they were also responsible for the preparation of the plan of Darod expulsion from the capital city Mogadishu.

I asked my brother the state of Darod clan and what it was doing to defend themselves. He said, "The Darod clan is not united to defend itself. Even though some Darod clans are struggling to defend themselves, other major Darod clans are not united yet. The Majeerteen clan positioned their militia at the Jirko-Official Club and the National Stadium. On the other hand, an Ogaden clan group took a position at and around Vanguard Militia Headquarters. But the main Ogaden militia of SPM is in Afgoe, and it is allied USC militia."

I asked him the position of Marehan and Dhulbahante clans, and what they were doing. "The Dhulbahante assembled their youth at the National Fairground, and the Marehan clan to a large extent are a part of government defenses. Marehan is not happy with the contribution of other Darod sub clans." He added, "The Marehan leaders are working with the regime, and they positioned their forces at 77 military camps, Hotel Taleh, 1st July Square and Villa Somalia. However, given the size of the USC forces and the resources they command, it seems the regime defense is like throwing a pocket of water at a burning forest."

I asked him what he heard about the SNM militia and the Rahanweyn clan. He said, "The SNM has been reported that it is help- ing the USC militia here in Mogadishu. It is also reported that some of its militia are operating the USC heavy equipment, including artillery pieces. The SNM is also active in the north of the country, where they are establishing local governments to pro- vide basic services to the public.

The conflict between the Somali Revolutionary government and the Isaq clan of Somaliland started long before the foundation SNM opposition movement in London. But long before the birth SNM, a group of Isaq professionals in Hargeisa established a voluntary organization called UFO, that performed social work. According to a member of the organization, the group wrote a letter to President Mohamed Siyad Barre requesting to allocate a portion of the Berbera port revenue to the Somaliland regions, namely Hargeisa and Burao or the Isaq people. They gave the letter to an Isaq minister who was at the time on visit in Berbera. The minister delivered the letter to the president, but the president sent back to Mr. Gani, who was the governor of Northeast provinces. It was reported, according to the members of the group, Mr. Gani passed the letter to Faisal, who was accused of being a regime spy. After Mr. Faysal's findings, most members of UFO were implicated in anti-regime activities, arrested and transferred to a jail in Mogadishu, and later they were given a lengthy jail time.

Following an alleged regime abuse of the Isaq clan by the So- mali regime, the clan dissidents, in particular, those residing in the Arab world and UK founded in 1981, the Somali National Movement (SNM) in London to overthrow the regime. It was not clear the role of the UK government in the formation of the SNM movement.

The Isaq clan claimed that the Somali regime responded harshly to the creation of SNM and instigated a ruthless military campaign against all members of the clan. The SNM movement accused the government of arbitrary arrests and summary executions and torture of its people. The movement blamed the regime of an indiscriminate bombing of Hargeisa city and the killing of thousand people, and the displacement of many people in 1988, who fled to Ethiopia. Between 1987 and 1989, the movement also recounted the massacring hundreds of members of the Isaq clan.

On the other hand, the leaders and population of the

Rahanweyn clan were not prepared to the sudden erup-
tion of the hostility and they just began organizing their
clan to shelled it from the fighting. It is rumored that
they were sympathetic to the USC cause. "

My brother was a committed Pan-Somalist, and it
seemed he was blind or refused to admit the anti-
Darod violence that had begun. In any case, from his
explanation, the polarization of So- mali clans into
rival camps was apparent. It was obvious the So- mali
nationalism and unity were shattered beyond salvation. It was also clear to me that a Somali civil war
was imminent and unavoidable.

****

Even though the leaders of the October Revolution
committed numerous mistakes, in hindsight, they ac-
complished some his- toric achievements. In 1974, the
Revolutionary government introduced a writing system
for the Somali language (Latin script). It became the official working language of the government and the
medium of instruction in all school levels.

Moreover, the government launched a nationwide
literacy campaign to teach the rural population how to
read and write. In 1974, all secondary schools and higher
education institutions in the country were closed for one
year, and teachers and students were sent to rural communities for the literacy campaign. By the end of 1975,
the campaign taught nearly two million of the rural population how to read and write the Somali language.

The Revolution made significant strides in economic
develop- ment. It introduced numerous programs for the
development of farming and livestock. In turn agricul-
ture production increased, and the livelihood of the rural

population improved. The Revolution also built several dozens of light factories to process agricultural products and manufacture consumer and construction supplies.

In 1969, when the military took power, the education level of the country was almost nonexistence. There were only a few primary and secondary schools in the state, and there were no higher education institutions except an Italian school in Mogadishu, which offered a few courses in Italian language and law. The Revolution built secondary schools in all regions of the country and inaugurated a primary school in all towns and villages. The Revolution also degreed the Somali language to be the medium of instruction in all school levels. It degreed the school enrollment of children at the age of six compulsory. The Revolution also founded a National University, encompassing all essential colleges in Mogadishu. Education was made free, including higher education, and a government job guaranteed to all college graduates.

When the military took power, the country had no health care service. The Revolution built hospitals and clinics in Mogadishu, all regional capitals, and districts that provided free health service to the population.

In 1974-75, a severe drought hit the North West region of the country. The land dried, livestock perished, the people became destitute, and a widespread famine followed the drought. When the news reached the Mogadishu, the revolutionary government rushed food, medicine, and water to the affected population and set relief camps.

The people in the drought area lost everything they had, and the government made a historic decision to resettle them to a stable environment in other parts of the country

and train them as farmers and fishers. The government employed 600 lorries, and 24 large planes and moved120,000
people from the drought region. It relocated them in three
farming areas along the Juba and Shabelle rivers and three
fishing towns on the Indian ocean coast. The relocated people trained as farmers and fishers, and within a short period,
self-sufficient communities emerged.

When the military took power, there were only a few
km of asphalt roads in the country. It took several weeks to
travel from one part of the country to another. The Revolutionary govern- ment built a network of paved roads, which
enabled the population to arrive at most destinations of the
country within hours.

Sadly, the Revolution drastically curtailed political
participation and denied human rights. As a result, the
people refused to defend 'the Glorious Revolution' when
it was invaded by the Ethiopia sponsored, clan-based
militias of USC, SSDF, SNM, and SPM, which were led
by power-hungry men.

Defending the Loot

Today the fighting resumed early, following the morning Prayer. After a week of turbulence and uncertainty, I decided to visit a friend, the Egyptian military attaché, to get a feel of the situation. I disguised myself by wearing a sarong and covering my head and face with a light turban. I entered my mother's room to see her before I leave the house. She looked at me, and for the first time in many days, she smiled and said, "You look like a camel boy!"

I laughed and said, "I am going back to my nomad roots!" When I told her and my sister, sitting with her, that I was going out, they were shocked. They besieged me to stay, but I insisted on leaving and promised them that I would be back soon.

My sister closed the door behind me, and I took the back alley of the African village where I lived. I quickly emerged at the junction of Sinai and Labor Roads on the 1st July Square. I saw a trail of exodus coming from the direction of Sinai Road. It was clear they were coming from the fighting area. The human trail stretched as far as the eye can see. Among the fleeing masses were elderly and women carrying bundles of their possessions and children on their heads and back, and some of them dragged along more children. Some of the moving masses included some who were pushing the older people in wheelbarrows. The sound of their shifting feet created a rhythm, which strangely seemed to generate energy and hope. The swaying human heads covered the road between 1st July Square and Digfer Hospital and be- yond. It seemed they were moving toward the Medina District. The urgency in their strides reminded me of scenes in films portraying wildlife escaping a bush fire. The people looked miserable and terrified. The only voice emanating from their nervous pro- cession was the cry of the children.

I joined the human flood. Some of them looked at me but turned away quickly and would not talk to me. Their stares were hollow as if they were gazing at an empty void. As we approached the Digger Hospital area, we heard gunfire coming from the direction of the Medina District. As we came closer, we saw security guards firing at groups of looters strolling aimlessly in the alleys of the vast compounds housing beautiful villas. It was apparent the looters were intent on invading the compounds and loot. The guards were on the top of the villas, and they unable able to hold the charging hooligans any longer.

The compounds were the residences of important people. Most of them were senior Somali Government officials and wealthy businessmen of various backgrounds, as well as the home of diplomats and embassies of foreign countries. The guards on the roofs were firing in the air in an attempt to repel the looters. It was apparent that those who ruled the country without check and balance, whose words were the law of the land, were facing the day of reckoning and were in a serious predicament. The thieves of the state were struggling to save their lives and what they robbed from the nation. I never dreamed I would see the day the 'untouchables', of the ruling class, who governed the country by impulse and assumed scary titles, would face the fury of the masses and the law of the jungle. No one thought the people who had commuted on chauffeur-driven limousines, who wore bow ties like newlywed, would be scared and hide holes like the rats. It was hard to believe the people who advised the President for 20 years not to share power, would be helpless and would be- come prisoners in their mansions. Their weaknesses were exposed in front of their families, who thought their men were 'godfathers'. I wondered how long the guards would hold back the angry and hungry mobs at their gates. The daring gangs were determined to get back some of what was stolen from them.

I drifted away from the mob, watching the unfolding drama and walked towards the home of my Egyptian friend, General Shawqi, the Egyptian military attaché to Somalia. His home amid beautiful villas occupied by embassies and some Somali elites. As I approached his house, I noticed the ground of many villas was covered with broken furniture, appliances, shattered household items, and numerous other trashed items. The doors and win- dows of some villas were missing or broken. It was clear the dwellings were abandoned, and the looters van- dalized them under cover of the dark. In the process, they had destroyed every- thing in their way in a calcu- lated act of revenge that suggested they were settling scores with the military junta that held the country hostage for decades. The damage was extensive, and the area looked like it had been hit by an earthquake, leaving only the fragrance of flowers coming from the terraced gardens.

I arrived at the gate of the general and knocked. A Somali man toting an AK-47 assault gun opened and looked back at the house for instruction. The gen- eral was watching us from the window of the second floor of the house and signaled the man to let me in. The general greeted me at the door of the villa and dragged me inside and took me to the living room. He looked tired and a bit confused. It seemed the uncer- tainty of the situation and the miss- ing of his govern- ment contacts worried him and drained his energy.

I knew the general for many years, met him regu- larly, and we discussed the politics of our countries and the world in general. Somalia was his first diplomatic as- signment, and I knew little of his background and did not ask him. I was not aware of any other responsibilities he held he carried in Somalia besides the military mat- ters. However, from our conversations, I surmised that he was trying to collect as much Somali information as he could, probably to establish a name for himself back home. Although most embassies pulled their staff out of Somalia soon after the conflict started, Egypt continued hanging on presumably to monitor the situation closely on the ground. However, the general was anxious to be evacuated for the safety of his wife and two children, who joined him a few months earlier on vacation. The conflict caught them, and I could hear their exasperated voices coming from the kitchen area.

The nicely furnished living room was turned into a war communication center certainly because of the fighting in the city. There were several machines with blinking lights in two corners of the room. We sat and a servant brought us tea. The general turned to me and said with some apprehension, "Tell me what is happening?"

Some years ago, I told the general that I studied African Government and Politics at SOAS and LSE of London University, and somehow mistakenly, he believed that I was an expert of African affairs. I tried many times to convince him that my knowledge of African politics is limited. But he continued to seek my opinion when a significant African issue emerges. At last, I stopped re- minding him of my ignorance of African politics, and I began to talk like an expert. I cleared my throat and said, "It seems Somalia is destroying itself, but I do not have enough information about the current situation." Then I said, "What do you hear from the diplomatic community?"

He began recounting horrifying incidents he received from the Diplotaxis. He said, "The regime bombarded all USC held positions, but USC militia and its supporters continue to capture many neighborhoods, including the Karan, Sinai, and Bondhere districts." He paused for a minute, then added, "I heard the USC is preparing to storm villa Somalia." Then he continued in a lament- ing voice, "I do not understand why! Why is Somalia destroying itself? Please tell me why?" I could not find prompt answers to his questions and could not dissipate his mounting anxiety. I assumed he was thinking of acceptable information to report back home to his superiors. Many Somalis believed their country fought Egypt's proxy with Ethiopia since its independence. The waters of the Blue Nile had been an ongoing source of tension be- tween Ethiopia and Egypt after Great Britain gave exclusive rights of the water to Egypt. Egypt had exploited the Somali dream of a Great Somalia and encouraged it to 'liberate' Somali- inhabited territory under Ethiopian rule. In 1964, during the presidency of Abdirashid A. Sharmarke, fighting broke out between Somalia and Ethiopia, and Egypt gave the Hakim13, a semi-automatic rifle to the Somali government. The gun helped the infant Somali army repulse the Ethiopian aggression but replaced by a Russian AK-47 automatic rifle. Although the Hakim rifle played a vital role in the Somali defense against the Ethiopian attack, the effectiveness of the gun was highly exaggerated.

The general checked his communication equipment, then interrupted my reverie and repeated his question, "Why on earth Somalia is on a mission of self-destruction?" Even though it was a self-reflection question, I looked at him and said, "Somalia has been digging its grave with the help of its friends for a long time. It seems we are witnessing its end as a nation. However, I do not understand why its Arab friends are not helping her in her hour of need?"

My comment surprised him, and he could not hide

his frustration. He fired back, "What do you want your Arab friends to do? The Somali regime is not communicating with us. Its army vanished overnight, and its civil service personnel joined their respective clan militias. Shockingly, the USC is buying ammunition, arms, and essential military supplies from the army depositories." He paused for a moment, and then added, "The Somali people as a whole are insignificant in the eyes of the world. I do not understand what they are trying to achieve by tearing their country into pieces."

The general had a point, and I did not want to argue with him. I knew some of the diplomatic community wished to remove the President from power and install individuals they trusted. But some members of the diplomatic community did not want rotten politicians who were tainted with greed and nepotism. It seemed the anti-regime members of the diplomatic community were not paying much attention to the rapidly deteriorating security situation of the country. They ignored the seriousness of the conflict, the possibility of civil war, and the significant influence of the clan politics in the Somali society.

Sadly, many diplomats had minimal contact with ordinary So- mali people and spent most of their time behind barricaded embassies and homes and moved from one banquet to another. They were only concerned with the number of days remaining for their stay in the country, and they had no interest in the furious fight- ing in the capital and the crisis the country was suffering.

I asked the general if the diplomatic community was interested in intervening or mediating the warring parts to prevent the looming disaster and to contain the conflict from spilling to the regions of the country. He quickly said, "The diplomatic community assigned the Italian and Egyptian ambassadors to en- gage the fighting parties, but USC leaders and other opposition move- ments refused to talk to the regime." He continued, "The USC leader, General Mo- hamed Farah Aydid, is not interested in talk- ing to the regime. The leaders of the SSDF, the SNM, and the SPM; Col. Abdullahi Yusuf, Mr. Abdirahman Toor, and Col. Ahmed Omar Jess, are not in Mogadishu and they could not be contacted." He paused briefly and then added, "On the other hand, it is difficult to find any regime representative with authority, and it is difficult to reach the President. Most of the regime senior officials are either hiding or already left the city." I asked him how the embassies found out that the senior people of the regime had fled and were not in the city. He said in a surprised tone, "They have their means!" And he added, "I think the senior offi- cials of the regime did not want to be identified with the Revolution anymore." He paused for several min- utes and sipped his tea and continued, "Anyway, the diplomatic community ex- change information, and some of the European countries and even some Arab countries are not interested in the Somali conflict. They think it is another episode in which African peo- ple cut each other throat when they cannot find a white person to slaughter."

I left the general late in the afternoon with a heavy heart. On my way home, I thought of the hopelessness of the situation I discussed with the general. The enor- mity of the challenges facing the country dawned on me

with full force. Many people wished the regime to vanish, but no one spared a thought for what would come
after the President and his system leave the scene.

The October Revolution of 1969 adapted Scientific
Socialism immediately after its birth and introduced
many changes in the education system of the country
and began to regulate and monitor the religious teachings. Notably, the changes greatly impacted the education system. New subjects with socialist content were
added to the curriculum, and a new school uniform was
introduced. The female students were required to wear
pants that were foreign to the culture and heads carves
were band in school settings.

The regime was also pressured by the Islamic movement in the country. In the early 1970s, many Somali
youths went to Saudi Arabia and the other Gulf States
for work. It was in the wake of the Middle East economic
boom, and the Somali economic immigrants worked at
the massive construction projects, in particular, in Saudi
Arabia. These job seekers came back in late 1970 with a
lot of money and a new Islamic ideology with Suadi
Arabia's sup-port. The returnees built new Mosques,
Koranic schools, and gradually an authoritarian form of
Islam began to take hold in Somalia and the Horn.
Some of the population accepted the new teachings, but
the followers of the traditional Sunni sect rejected the
Saudi Arabia influence.

The Somali regime, led by the October Revolution
of 1969, felt threatened by the new Islamic ideology
and took measures to minimize its impact. It sided with
the traditional Sunni branch of Islam, which rejected
the new Islamic teachings propagated from Suadi Ara-

bia, and the regime began to monitor the activities of mosques and the Islamic schools supported by Suadi Arabia.

The austere teachings of Islam support in the country, and the government was forced to establish new defenses against the growing anti-establishment Islamic influence. It raised the status of the Sunni sheikhs and their followers and promoted it to the status of the state religion.

Previously the Revolution led by General Mohamed Said Barre introduced numerous laws that were mostly welcomed by society. He banned tribalism, banned Qat, instituted employment for those without jobs, made women enlist in the military, pro- moted the status of low-caste sections of the society, including the Midgan, Tumal, Bantu and promoted them to the highest government positions. But he made a grave mistake, that eventually brought down his rule, when he declared that 'men and women are equal'. The declaration mobilized both Sunni and non-Sunni Islamic forces against the Revolutionary government and ousted the revolutionary regime with the help of the pseudo opposition movements that were already fighting it.

On June 26 and July 1, 1960, the blue Somali flag with white star at the center was raised on free Somali soil.

(1529-1543) Amir Ahmed bin Ibrahim al-Ghazi campaigned against the Abassynian expansion to south into his Sultanate of Adal. Amir Ahmed defeated several Abyssinian emperors during the campaign and in the process brought three-quarters of Abyssinia proper under the rule of the Somali Sultanate of Adal. The campaign ended when the crusade army of Christian Europe led by Portuguese joined the war on the Abyssinian side. Amir Ahmed was killed by a Portuguese sniper.

Sayid Mohammad Abdullah Hassan was one of Africa resistance leaders. He founded and led the Dervishes movement (1899-1920), which fought the colonial powers that divided the Somali inhabited territory into five parts. He is the father of Somali nationalism and founder of Somali state, which was recognized by several governments, including Ottoman and German governments of his time.

#

1943

This is logo of the Somali Youth League (SYL), founded in 1943. In 1960, the League achieved the independence of two portions of the Somali inhabited territories. Later, the League became a political party, and won the national elections of 1960 and 1969. During its reign, the party was ravaged by corruption and tribalism, and it was ousted by the military coup of October 21, 1969.

PM Abdullahi Issa Mohamud (1921 – 1988) served in the Central Committee of SYL. Later, he was selected as the first Prime Minister of Somalia (February 29, 1956 to July 1, 1960) when the country was placed under the United Nation trusteeship (1950 -1960). He could not run for the office of the President because of his age. After the independence, he served his country as foreign minister and ambassador to Italy. As PM, he served his country honorably, and many Somalis respect him for his integrity, decency, and for not tempting to usurp the presidency at the independence in 1960.

| Pre. A. Osman | Pre.A.A. Shararke | PM A. H. Hussen | PM. M I. Igal |

The leaders of the Somali Republic (1960-1969), failed to foster a democratic political rule and were overwhelmed by clan politics. At the end of their reign in 1969, there were more than 84 clan-based political parties in the country. They were ousted by the clan politics that in the first place propelled them to power.

Col. Abdalla   Gen. Samatar   Pre. Siad   Gen. Afrah   Col. Farah

(1969-1991) The members of the Politburo of the Central Committee of October 21, 1969 coup, in attempt to eradicate tribalism from society, introduced alien ideology of Scientific Socialism to Somalia political system, and altered the Somali social fabric. At the end, they were sucked by the clan politics they were trying to stamp out. The Revolution was ousted by politically bankrupt and clan minded opposition groups.

Col. A. Yusuf   Gen . Moh.Aydid   Mr. A. Y. Ahmed   Col . Ahmed O.J ees

(1989 - ?) Some fake heroes of Somali clans who founded clan based opposition militias in Ethiopia, misled their clans to gain power. They entombed the Somali unity and nationalism, and I will not be surprised if their misguided clans erect for them statues.

January 8, 1991
Mogadishu, Somalia

The King is Dead

The voice of my mother praying awoke me early in the morn- ing. She was supplicating God for health, forgiveness, deliverance, and paradise afterlife. My mother broke her neck 15 years ago, and she was paralyzed below the neck and could only move her head, and was bedridden. But she loved life and laughed, and continued to be as happy as any other healthy person before the war broke out in the city.

I entered her room and sat on the edge of her bed to comfort her. The worry in her eyes was overwhelming, and my smiles could not overcome her anxiety. My sister brought us tea, and we sipped the tea with some dates. We talked about fighting, and I told them my intention to visit the Bakaraha market, the biggest in the country, to buy food. They began to worry and tried to pre- vent me from going out, but I insisted on leaving. Since the city lost all communications, it was impossible to know what was happening beyond our front doors. I did not know the situation in the market, and who took control of it since my last   visit.

As soon as I left the house in disguise, I bumped into Abdi, a relative of my wife, who came to check on us. He worked at Radio Mogadishu of the Ministry of Information, and I had not seen him since I was removed from my position as the managing director of Somali National Television and stopped going to the Ministry. He was aware of USC activities and the situation at the Ministry. We walked together to the main street and exchanged the information we had about the fighting. He jokingly said, "You have not come to the Ministry for some time, and maybe your name has been added to the list of the deserters who joined the opposition groups?"

I laughed and said, "I have no job! And the opposition has not hired me yet!"

He accusingly said, "Some Hawiye employees at the Ministry are acting as though they are loyal to the regime, but they are working for USC. They are not sure of the future and the outcome of the conflict."

I thought of the government's difficult situation. Maybe, Abdi was right, and the regime was disconcerted, and even it can't re- member who works for it. Perhaps it believes anyone who did not report for the defense of the 'Blessed Revolution' was a traitor or a deserter. In reality, no one wanted to be associated with the regime anymore. Death was hovering over everyone, including the 'Father of the Nation.' I asked myself, "Who are they to call people deserters if people refuse to come out to kiss death?"

Abdi was from Majeerteen clan, but his mother was Hawiye. He was among the haunted before the regime lost its grip on power because of his clan affiliation. He had lived with his mother's clan, and stayed at the Ministry, even though most of Darod employees left the Ministry for fear. Only the Hawiye employees who were USC supporters remained with the Ministry of Information, waiting for the collapse of the regime.

Out of concern for my family, Abdi said, "The safety of the city is rapidly deteriorating. You must take out the family before it is too late!" He paused for a moment and then added, "I can hang on for a while with my mother's clan, but I do not see any cover for you!" His talk reminded me of Somali wisdom, which states that 'a father helps his son only once, and that is when he espouses his mother.'

He continued telling me the situation at the Ministry, "They forced all the Darod employees out all departments of the Ministry. Now only a few Darod workers who have Hawiye connections stayed there. They even hunted down senior Darod managers and collected the keys of their offices, including Terra, the Managing Director of Somali Broadcasting Corporation."

I asked Abdi if any Darod senior officers had visited the Ministry since the fighting started. He was not sure, and could not tell anyone who came back. Again, I asked about the USC and regime activities. He said that he heard an ongoing meeting of Somali elders and government officials and a group calling them- selves Manifesto. He added, "I heard that the Manifesto group has been meeting the government since May 1990, and it is planning to meet the president soon." He added, "The Manifesto group includes individuals from most of the Somali clans, and it is led by important individuals, including Ali Shido Abdi Omar, Dr. Ismail Jimale, Mr.

Hashi Weheliye, Haji Muse Boqor, and other influential individuals."

We parted with the encouraging Manifesto news, which offered a flicker of hope of the future. I thought if there were any hope left for peace, it might come from the Manifesto group. Even though the Somali people respected the authority of the titled traditional leaders more than any other group, many of them were not in the Manifesto group. Even though many people did not trust the regime, they also believed several members of the Manifesto group were cor- rupt, self-serving, and unrepresentative. I continued my walk toward Bakaraha Market. It was not far from my house, and the streets and alleys were deserted. When I came closer to the market, I heard a commo- tion, which grew louder as I approached the edge of the market. Then came into my view a large crowd that formed a circle and dancing. The participants were clenching their firsts and shot in the air contin- uously. From their chanting, it was clear they were USC supporters.

It seemed most of the dancing people were market watchmen. In the market, there were no many shoppers, and apparently, its closing was imminent because of the fighting. At the entrance of the market, from one of the alleys, young men with rifles came out and stopped me. One of the men came closer and started questioning me. I could hear one of the other men saying, "Check for an ID! Maybe he is a spy!" Another man added, "Who knows, it could be our lucky day!" They were stopping and searching all the people entering the market. It was clear they were USC men. It seemed they were on the lookout for the regime or Darod people. I was sure if they found out my clan, I would be harassed. They let the people enter the market in order not to antagonize the few merchants who dared to open their businesses and needed shoppers to feed their families.

The market was the most important in the country, and it had massive warehouses, large stores, small factories, and a wide-open market. It supplied the markets central and south of the country and neighboring countries.

In the market, most stalls were not attended and were covered with rags. Only a few people were there selling some dry food. Among them were few older women and children accompanying some of them. They were selling beans, corn, and some other dry and canned food. There were no vegetables, fruits, milk, or meat. I was not sure whether the traders had boycotted the market in support of the USC or were frightened and stayed away. I turned to one of the women in the corner of the market after our eyes met, and she smiled. Two children were playing on her back, and I thought, 'She has to feed these children who don't understand the crisis in their city, and the bleak future that awaits them.' I greeted the woman, looked at her goods, and I asked her what happened traders of the market.

She forced a smile and replied, "They will be back when the fighting is over." Then she looked at me directly in the eye and added, "You should know what is happening! All the men have gone to join the fighting."

I was not sure what she was thinking. I thought,' Maybe she suspected that I am Darod!' I began to justify my ignorance, "I have been sick lately, and I care for my bedridden mother. I am aware of the fighting but could not join the struggling brothers because of my health and sick mother."

She was sympathetic, "May Allah give both of you quick health! By the will of God, the situation will change as soon as we liberate ourselves and our city!"

I changed the subject to avoid suspicion: "I am looking for fresh vegetables and milk for my mother."

She informed me, "Vegetables have not arrived for many days. The Afgoe road is closed, and the truck drivers who brought the produce are afraid of the fighting."

I expressed my understanding of the situation, "It will be over soon, and the situation will return to normal for all of us to earn our daily bread without fear!"

She began to pay tribute to the USC militia and the clan fight- ers. "Yes!" She said, "The gallant fighters are winning the fight, and soon we will be in power...."

I bought some beans and corn from her and walked away quickly. The chanting of the dancing crowd followed me. They repeated the words of an older man at the center of the circle, who chanted and led the dance. He glorified the USC militia and its 'heroic' struggle. He appealed to all Hawiye people to support the movement. The crowd repeated his words and jumped high in the air and pounded the ground hard with their feet, generating a cloud of dust. The chanting, jumping and clapping produced a thumping rhythm for the dance as the older man continued his exhortations, and the crowd responded:

Older man: USC!

The crowd: Long live!

The older man: The Eagle! (General Aydid)

The crowd: Long live!

The older man: Victory! The crowd: USC!

The older man: Who liberated us?

The crowd: USC!

I covered my head with the turban and continued quietly drifted away from the market. What surprised was the excitement of the dancers and the jubilant cele-bration of Somali people on June 26 and July 1, 1960, after two of the Somali inhabited terri- tories received their independence from Great Britain and Italy, respec-tively. I asked myself whether Somalia was a nation in crisis or several nations fighting to be independent of each other. I mused over the 'relief' the crowd was ex-pecting from the USC if it wins the fight.

I returned home safely and gave the beans and corn to my sister to cook. I entered my mother's room. She looked at me with worried eyes. I wished her peace and then asked her how she feels.

"Thanks to God!" she said and quickly turned her face away to hide her worries. I said, to comfort her, "The fighting will stop soon. Some Somali politicians and eld-ers, including Haji Muse Boqor are expected to meet the President."

She looked at me and said, "Who is talking to the fighting people? What do they want?"

Her question took me by surprise. I was not sure what to say. 'Who is talking to the fighting groups?' I thought the President held the key to the solution of the conflict, and I expected he would invite the leaders of the opposition militias, the Somali eld- ers, and would sit with them to avert the apparent calamity.

My mother repeated the question, "Who is talking to the fighting people?"

The question brought me back from deep thoughts. I said un- surely, "I think the president and the Somali elders will talk to them."

My mother understood very little about the con- voluted Somali tribal politics. However, her question reminded me of the stark reality of the conflict. She understood the old clan warfare, which had revolved around livestock raids, grazing land, and water re- sources. In those old days, they used only spears, dag- gers, and arrows, and only a few men were killed in a day fighting. Unfortunately, in the recent Somali fighting, modern firearms were used, and hundreds of people killed in minutes. Unlike the old days, con- temporary clan warfare was an attempt to control the nation's meager resources. It was a fight between in- dividuals who exploited the emotions of their clans to grab the seat of power and the benefits and opportu- nities that came with it. My mother was right to ques- tion the wisdom of the militia leaders! 'Who is talking to the Hawiye, Isaq and Darod and the others in- volved in the fighting? Who is talking to clans who were misled, mobilized and thinking they were de- fending the 'honor' of their respective clans? Who holds the key to peace?'

My mother was a brilliant woman, but she was living in challenging and times, and she could not comprehend what was happening. She usually suggested a solution to all family problems. I remember one night, a long time ago, when all the family gathered in her room and watched a football game on television. For her, it was the first time she watched a TV and the game. She could not understand why 22 grown men were running after each other and fought over a small round thing (ball). She asked me what they were doing, and I explained to her the game and its rules. After she watched and thought over for some time, she asked, "Why they do not take the ball in turns and allow each group to score as many goals as they want?" It seemed the 'fight' between the regime and the opposition militia was meaningless, like the grown men trying to drive a small round thing between two poles.

My sister brought us the food she cooked, and my younger brother, who came from the city, joined us. He brought horrifying news, which shattered the little hope we expected from the meet- ing between the President and the Manifesto group. He told us that a shell landed on a vehicle carrying some of the manifesto group, and several elders, including Haji Muse Boqor and Hashi Weheliye, were killed.

As soon as the shocking news spread in the city, the number of people leaving North to Medina District in the south increased. Later that evening, more people in my area began to load their possessions on trucks, cars, donkey carts, and leave. No one dared to venture out of their homes after sunset.

The expectation of the people from the meeting of the Manifesto group and the President to achieve peace dwindled. Many of the manifesto group were members of the previous civilian ad- ministration ousted in 1969 by the ruling military regime. Among them were also several prominent businessmen who carried little weight. Some of the Manifesto group were senior managers and ministers at the eve of the coup in 1969. They were imprisoned for many years and held grudges against President Siad Barre and the regime. Women were not included in the Manifesto group and top people in the administration. Haji Muse Boqor, in particular, was a parliamentarian and leading contender to be- come the next President of the Republic, following the assassination of the sitting President Dr. Abdirashid A. Sharmarke in the town of Las'anod.

I heard from different sources, the President suspected the neutrality of the Manifesto group, after it became known that the group secretly works with the leaders of the militias. Indeed, many people questioned the group's intentions, since some of its members exhibited animosity towards the President and the regime and supported opposition groups without questioning their agenda. It seemed the Manifesto group lucked credibility and missed the opportunity to mediate the government, and the opposition group to stop the fighting because of their tainted background.

There was conflicting information on the assassination of some of the Manifesto elders. Some people pointed the finger at the regime, but it was not easy to prove whether they were assassinated by the regime or by the USC. In any case, it was a severe blow to the group's initiative to achieve a negotiated settlement. Another scary and dark night covered the city. The only visible light was the flares of the gunfire in the sky. Uncertainty and fear continued to hang over the city, and the people anxiously awaited the light of another day and prayed the conflict to end.

January 9,1991
Mogadishu, Somalia

Time to Call God

After many days of bitter fighting, it was relatively quiet late in the morning when the fight started again. The communication in the city was nonexistent, and people depended on word of mouth for the news of the day. Although it was not safe, I left home at noon to pray at the neighborhood mosque.

A few people, with hollow gazes, hurried in all directions, and streets were deserted. The usual crowds of people who roamed the streets were gone. The multitude of cars, which sped through the streets, as though they were escaping an approaching bush fire, had disappeared. Occasionally, one or two people would emerge from the alleys and quickly went into another alley.

The air was heavy with the smell of burning gunpowder and debris. The explosions coming from downtown subdued the sound of whirling wind and the clatter of the swinging windows. A few animals occasionally darted around aimlessly, bewildered and frightened by the sudden change that altered their peaceful environment.

I arrived at the mosque, hoping to find someone I knew. I re- moved my shoes at the door and entered tip-toeing gently.

A few men were waiting for the call of noon prayer. Some looked at me inquiringly as though I had the news of the fighting. I went to a bookshelf on one of the walls containing old and unorganized copies of the Quran. I pulled a copy and sat in a corner, and began reading it silently. Suddenly, I remember the warnings of some of the sheiks who preached that 'unbelievers remember God when they are scared, and they ask for salvation and forgiveness. They remember God only when they are close to their destruction.'

After I read a few verses of the Holy Book, I closed it and looked around again. Most of the attendants sat in groups and were engaged in an intense discussion. The conversation of some of the groups sounded like an argument and conveyed nervous- ness.

The atmosphere of the mosque lacked the typical mosque meditative ambiance, in which attendees quietly read the Quran. The gazes and facial expressions of the congregation generated a feel- ing of fear that negated the usual serenity that permeated from a mosque congregation before the prayer. The beams of light that came through the window cracks added to the inescapable unease.

I leaned back and closed my eyes. I wanted to be invisible, and I wished I had wings to fly away to a far-away place, far from the madness and uncertainty that engulfed the city and the normal life. I wished I had no responsibility for anything, even for myself. I wished the wait for the prayer to continue forever.

The call of the imam for the prayer brought me back from a deep contemplation that took me to another planet. I stood with others, and we formed lines and began praying, following the recitation of the imam and repeating the verses he read. Some- times, instead of listening and paying attention to the imam with complete submission to God, I drifted away, thinking about the danger my family was facing.

After the imam ended the first part of the prayer, he sat facing us with folded legs and raised his hands to the ceiling, blessing the nation and the Muslim believers. We followed him, adding 'Amin' to every verse he mentioned. He glorified God and appealed for help and said, "... O, Lord! We seek your guidance and Your mercy. We ask You to bestow Your glory upon us as You decree since You know what the future holds for us! Help us God, and strengthen our faith. O, God! Pardon our sins, for we are naive, and guide us in the right path. O, God! Do not punish us for our sins. God! Save us from our bad deeds, for we are weak and defenseless. You are.... Amen." He concluded.

I contrasted the imam's blessing with the beliefs of the Ituri Forest people14 of Central Africa, who believe that all lives on the planet are connected and interdependent. Their belief puts a man in the center of the universe, with the responsibility of protecting people, animals, and plants equally. For a man to perform his duties, he must be clean, spiritually, and physically. The followers of this belief do not expect help from their deities for the problems they bring upon themselves. They bear responsibility for the trouble that impacts the lives of people, animals, and plants that man was entrusted to protect. Unlike the true heavenly Semitic religions, this belief did not expect gods to send messengers when calamity struck them. I left the mosque and returned home without good news for my mother.

I lived in the African village, a gated compound that encompassed dozens of apartment blocks. The government built the compound for the OAU conference, which was held in Mogadishu in 1974. It housed the low-level members of the conference delegations. After the end of the African conference, the apartments were rented to mid-level government officials.

Since the start of the conflict, I met friends who lived in my neighborhood, and we exchanged the news and information of the day. We joked and teased each other to ease the harsh reality we were facing. We discussed the current events and the political situation of the country, including the ongoing fighting. The artillery vibration from afar punctuated our conversation. Today, only two of my friends, Mohamed and Mahdi came to my place. We exchanged what each of us heard regarding the fighting. Mohamed said, "It is strange! We have not heard anything from the opposition, in particular, the USC. I think they ought to inform the public and explain their mission and political program if they have one!"

I asked him, "How do you want them to do it? They have no means of informing the public. They cannot even print a   flyer!"

"That is not a justification!" he responded. "They can create neighborhood watch committees in the areas they control and can inform and organize the people."

"The USC created committees in many neighbor-hoods long ago before the fighting started," I quickly corrected him. I added, "It seems the USC is not interested in some neighborhoods. Any- way, there is a rumor that the USC militia is in the process of forming a national government headed by general Aydid."

In a surprised voice, Mohamed countered, "Are you saying at this early stage, the USC is contemplating forming a govern- ment?"

"That is what I heard," I replied. I added, "Anyway if the USC wants to replace the 'blessed Revolution' I think that is the logical outcome of the conflict. But USC must realize that Somalia cannot have a government without the blessing of Darod."

"That is an offensive joke!" Mohamed said with dismay. He added, "USC can't form a government alone which is acceptable to all the Somali people!"

Mahdi joined the conversation and suggested the possibility of USC regime, "Why not?" He said, "They believe that the Darod formed past Somali regimes since 1960 without consulting the So- mali people!"

"That is not true!" Mohamed interjected. "Even the Supreme Revolutionary Council of 1969 was inclusive, and the affiliation of the 25 council members included most of the Somali clans. Even the so-called minorities were included, and the second man of the Revolutionary Council since October 21, 1969, General Mohamed Ali Samater is from the minority clans ." Then he added, "Sadly, for an unknown reason, some of the minority, in particular, Digil/Mirifle clan, was not represented in the Revolutionary Council. Maybe they had no senior officers in the army at the birth of the Revolution." He continued, "Anyway, I think USC alone cannot form a national government. USC must at least in- vite the other opposition groups, the SSDF, the SNM, and the SPM to join it before even it considers of forming a government." I refused to accept his suggestion, "Forget the SNM! It is not interested in Somalia, and it will be busy 'cleaning' the non-Isaq population from the so-called 'British land' for a long time to come. The Isaq clan does not trust Darod, and I think it does not respect the tribes in the south of the country (Italian Somaliland)." I tried to explain, further, the problem facing any attempt of forming a Somali government, "Anyway I said, the SSDF also does not want to share power with other Somali clans. It believes it is the movement that brought down the 'Blessed Revolution', and it has the right to replace its leaders." I continued my argument, " All opposition movements are clan-based, and they do not trust each other. That is their Achilles heel!"

Our friend Mahdi, who quietly and respectfully listened to most of our arguments, rejoined the discussion. He said, "I do not understand the mess we are in! Sadly, lawlessness and untamed youth murdering each other, and the innocent people are uproot- ing our society. They call themselves liberation movements, and they are led by ailing men who are in quest of power, and only they know how to turn our youth into killing machines! At any rate, the world does not care about Somalia, and I do not under- stand what the USC and other opposition groups are trying to achieve by destroying the country."

I agreed, "I do not understand either! Maybe we need Professor Goran Hyden15 to explain it to us!"

Mohamed jumped in, "Why Professor Hyden?

Our scholars can explain the problem, and they can find a solution."

Mahdi disagreed, "Oh God! Our scholars are part of the prob- lem. They live in foreign capitals, and they talk to each other through their writings, and do not care about the suffering of their people." Mahdi continued, "The common man is invisible to them, and in fact, many of them are lighter than their shadows.

They enhance their names with fancy prefixes and suffixes such as Dr., Professor, Ph.D., Eng., etc. to show their superiority to the rest of us." He added, describing the Somali elite, "I think some of our so-called scholars love themselves so much, they are out- side the realm of reality. Sometimes they talk like the Prophet Moses, and they sound as though they wish to take their clans to the 'promised land'. Some of them unknowingly contribute to clannish politics and are laboring to revise Somali his- tory to prove that their clans are different nations with identifiable characters. Some 'professors' are in search of 'the Imaginary Nation' between the two rivers."

Mohamed laughed hysterically and countered Mahdi by say- ing, "You are telling us strange stories! Where did you read all these hilarious stories? The Somalis are the only homogeneous people in Africa, and their shared experience is widely documented. By the way, we have not mentioned the role of Somali politicians."

We laughed and then Mahdi said, "If we have politi- cians, why they are not solving our problems? Why they do not lead the people and prevent the destruction our nation is undergoing? I think the people we are calling politicians are self-appointed idiots who thrive on the misery of their helpless people."

It got dark, and I told my friends to go home, "Let us pray for peace. Nothing can be worse than Somalis killing each other. I question the patriotism of the opposition groups. Without a doubt, they are directed by our traditional enemy Ethiopia."

"I Agree!" Mahdi said and added, "Praying to God to save us is the only remaining hope for us! By the way, I think we should not blame President Siyad Barre and his government. We have been telling the 'old man' for the last 20 years that he is an exceptional leader in Africa, and unfortunately, he believes it and he will never relinquish the power to save people even from the hell- fire! He is the Nero of Somalia."

I said, "I think we must blame the so-called opposition groups led by power-hungry lunatics who are destroying everything in their path like an uncontrollable fire." We all agreed and departed.

I met US Ambassador to Somalia (1982- 1984), Mr. Robert B. Oakley in his office after I received Parvin fellowship to study at Woodrow Wilson Public and Interna-tional Afairs, Princeton University in New Jersey, USA.

(1981-1982) Parvin Fellowship Program participants from Nepal, China, Bangaladesh, Philippines, India and Somalia and the program administrators at School of Woodrow Wilson Public and International Affairs, Princeton University.

The Egyptian Military Attache General Shawqi and I at his home the day he departed Somlia to Egypt in January 1991.

My uncle Haji Farah Haid who raised me. He was a well-known businessman in Ethiopia. He died in 1965.

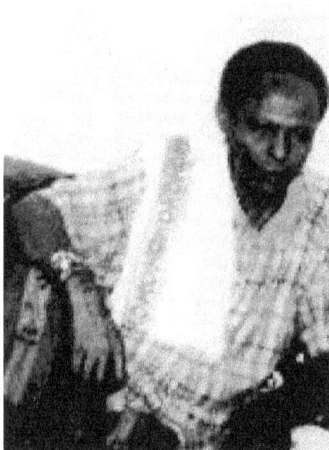

My brother Abdi and his only son Hassan Abdi. Both were murdered by USC militia in January 1991 in Mogadishu.

From Camel Herding to College

The fighting between the USC movement and regime forces continued at a low intensity. The government re- treated from sev- eral strategic locations, and USC moved in them quickly. If the regime continues to aban- don the critical fronts it held, it was clear the USC militia would ultimately capture the whole city.

Every passing day heightened my worry and con- cern for my family. I could not sleep most nights, and I stayed awake thinking about the future of my family. I usually jumped out of bed when I hear the call of Morn- ing Prayer to go to the mosque.

Last night was a worry-loaded night for me, and I spent toss- ing and turning in my bed, my mind was full of turmoil and anxious thoughts. I could not find an an- swer to any of my problems. The past flooded back on me with a vengeance. It reminded me of the time I wasted and the numerous worthy things I was leaving behind unfinished. I remembered the countless opportu- nities I denied myself and my family and the prospect of having a better life. The unnecessary choices I made in the past and the possibilities I refused my loved ones, and sad thoughts swamped my head. I did not worry for myself or my wife and children or my brothers and sisters. I worried for my bedridden mother, who broke her neck many years ago.

My father married my mother in the year 1950s. They had lived in a rural community, and raised camel, goat, and sheep. My father died from a snake bite after fathering five children from her – four boys and one girl. I was the second child, and my sister was the youngest. We were between the ages of two and eight at the time of his death.

We had a wonderful childhood in the rural community. We drank milk in the morning and followed the grazing animals all day. We kept watchful eyes on the animals anticipating the canny foxes and other beasts from killing them. We killed lizards rab- bits, dikdik, rabbits, and other small animals using bows and arrows we made from twigs. We played games, and when the sun gets hot, we sat under a tree or anthill and curved the shape of our animals from dry clays lifted from the base of the anthills. We extracted honey stored in trees and rocks by bees, ant, and wasps, etc. Using grass straws, we quenched our thirst with the rainwater stored in tree trunks. In the evening, after we bring the animals safely home, we played many games, including tag and hid, stick throwing, etc. We were given for dinner milk, dates and sorghum soaked in ghee and milk and occasionally a boiled or baked meat. It was the happiest time of my life.

Following the death of my father, a severe

drought hit the community, which later ushered a famine called Red Dust (Siigo Case), and my family lost all its livestock. For a time, we lived on the generosity of our relatives. The drought lingered and brutalized the community and approximately annihilated their livestock. A strong wind blew, and it appeared it carried all the soil on the ground and flung it into the air and turned the sky red. The people walked with difficulty, covering their faces and rubbing their eyes continuously to clear the dust. All the trees died or turned into lifeless, brittle twigs and dry wood. All the water sources in the area dry, and the grazing land turned into a barren desert. Most of the sup-port we were receiving from our relatives stopped after the community's livestock perished.

The famine persisted, and the people began to die. The community decided to travel to the closest water source –Ainaba[16], which was about 100 km from where we were in Haud. Around 1955, the people embarked on a trek of many days, driving the remainder of their livestock.

Both the people and animals were frail, and when they could not walk anymore, they stopped abruptly, lay down on the ground, and died, and the skeleton of dead animals littered the trail. Many people died, and those who survived had no energy to bury them, and they wrapped their body with tattered clothes, dry twigs and placed them on the tops of tall, dry, and standing trees to prevent the scavengers from devouring them.

Every day at sunset, we camped for night rest. We had nothing to eat and chewed the roots of trees collected by my mother to moisten our dry throats and fill our bellies. One evening, my mother decided to feed us with the flesh of a corpse of an animal left to die on the road. She skinned it, cut its meat, and put it on a glowing fire to bake. Four of us huddled together near the fire, eagerly waiting for the meat, as my mother inspected it and continued turning it repeatedly. We followed her moves, and when she finally placed the meat on dry twigs in front of us, we jumped on it and tore it into pieces and stuffed in our mouths. We could not swallow the meat. It was so emaciated, tasteless, and smelled like a decaying wood. We tossed it out and slept with empty stomachs.

At last, after traveling for many days, we arrived at Ainaba artesian well, which was on a vast plain covered with dunes. There were hundreds of people and thousands of animals, form- ing a queue to slake their thirst. A vast number of water pots dis- mounted from camels surrounded the mouth of the well to be filled for the voyage back to the outfield areas where the remain- ing livestock could graze on dry leaves until the rainy season arrives. The children drank the water until their kidneys hurt, and then they were sent to watch over the animals.

There were hundreds of herds comprising thou- sands of heads, which come from all over the country. It was a problem keeping herds separated, and if an animal strays, it was difficult to recover it. Sadly, since none of our animals survived, we watched the flocks of our relatives.

Without livestock, my mother couldn't raise us in rural. She left us with close relatives and went to the city to get help from our family members who lived in the cities. After weeks, she re- turned with many beautiful gifts, including a pair of children's sandals, which I liked very much, and money to buy animals, but she also told us that she was taking some of us to our relatives in the city. She said the child that takes the beautiful sandals would stay with her in the rural when others travel to the city to live with their relatives. I asked about the availability of water in the city, and she assured me that I would drink water whenever I wanted. I gave the sandals to my older brother and decided to go to the city. If I had decided to keep the sandals, I would have ended as a camel man today.

My mother left my oldest brother and youngest sister with relatives and carried three of us from the Buuhoodle area to Burao town in northern Somalia. We had not seen a city before but heard they were places in which people lived in permanent homes with burning lamps at night. We also heard that the people did not keep animals. However, what excited me most was the promise of the abundance of water and food, and freedom from starvation.

In Burao, a distant relative who lived in a hut on the edge of the town received us. We rested for a few days, and then took an- other truck to Berbera, where my cousin, who was married to Omar, the CEO of ABC Company, lived. We arrived in the city in the evening, and I was amazed by the huge buildings. They were much bigger than anthills, which were common in rural areas. We were also surprised by the burning lamps hanging from the buildings and streets posts. The house of my cousin was on the edge of the sea, and the vast pool (the sea) amazed us. We wondered about the spaciousness of the sea, which covered the land as far as the eye could see. The waves invading the land scared us, and I asked my mother if the rain had left the vast pool and the waves rushing to conquer the dry land overnight. The explanation of my mother could satisfy my curiosity, and she could only explain the half-naked people in the water and big lizards (fish) they were taking out of the water. I wished the people I had left behind in the bush, where every drop of water was as precious as gold, would have similar pools. I believed my mother when she told me I would never be thirsty again.

My mother asked my cousin to keep my youngest brother, mother, and two us continued our trip to Harar in Ethiopia, where my uncle Haji Farah Haid, a businessman and later the Minister at Ministry of Interior of Ethiopia resided. In Harar, my uncle lived in a large compound with many servants and had many cars, lorries, and other strange machines. We were received kindly, and he gave us a place and comfort we thought never existed.

According to Somali customs, my uncle was required to marry my mother, but that was not possible because of their difference in social status and lifestyle. After he gave her what seemed to me a lot of money, she left me with his family and went the remaining boy all the way to Mogadishu, where my sister from a different mother lived. My sister was married to Mr. Ahmed Umal, aka Alore, a member of the SYL executive board. My mother left the boy with the sister to be there raised, and went back and joined my oldest brother and my youngest sister in the Haud and Reserved Area. She bought some animals with the money she collected from our relatives and continued to raise her two children in Haud. She married again and gave birth to a child who died at a young age.

In the cities, we all were enrolled in schools, studied hard, and graduated from colleges. Thanks to our mother's kindness and ingenuity, we got jobs and became successful. I believed if the op- position movements; and the regime consulted my mother, she would have given them a sensible solution to the Somali conflict. I thought she was a better thinker and problem solver than the fighting gentlemen who decorated their shoulders and chests with shining metals to emulate their colonial masters.

After the death of my uncle, Haji Farah 1965, I got a scholar- ship to attend the King's Royal Boarding school of Kotobe. After my graduation from high school in 1969, I planned to attend Haile Selassie University. But the student unrest in Addis Ababa, that against the government of Haile Selassie, which began after the aborted coup of the Imperial Guards led by general Mengistu Neway of 1961 gathered momentum and the security in Addis Ababa, became dangerous. In 1970, I moved to Mogadishu, So- malia, where I joined my two brothers and many other family members. My other brother, sister, and mother, who remained in the country, also joined us in Mogadishu a few years later. The boys attended universities in Somalia abroad and one of them , Dr. Mohamud Mohamed Haid studied medicine at Somali, American, and Italian universities and became a famous surgeon. He operated heart in 1988 in Digfer Hospital in Mogadishu. We were all hired by the Somali Central government and lived hap- pily in Mogadishu.

My mother broke her neck in an accident and became paralyzed. She lived with me, and we lived a stable life until the fight exploded in Mogadishu. My mother saved us from the harsh nomadic life after my father died, and a severe drought hit the community. It was our turn to care for her and protect her from the unpredictable and volatile situation created by the fighting of the dying regime and the clan-based opposition militias that made us prisoners in our own home.

That day in the afternoon, I decided to visit my friend, General Shawqi, to find out the news of the fighting and the political momentum in the city. When I arrived at his home, he received me at the door and took me to his living room, where several former and current senior government officials were sitting. We greeted each other warmly, and then the general invited me to join them. He introduced me to the group, as though we were meeting for the first time. I knew most of the men – Col. Mohamed, who worked at the Sayid Mohamed Abdulle Hassan Academy, where I taught African politics, Ambassador Sharif, Col. Nero, and others whom I knew for a long time. After an aimless, rambling talk, General Shawqi wanted to know what we were thinking. He mentioned a few events which some of us already knew, and then one of the generals in the group asked the general if he heard any new proposals from the international community or the govern- ment. It was embarrassing for the members of the Somali elite to ask foreigners the political situation of their own country. Nothing was expected from the International Community to tell the warring parties.

The general turned to me and asked me if there were

any suggestions for stopping the fighting. I surveyed the people in the room and said, "I think some of the most senior Somali officials are here with us in this room, and they can better explain to us why we are fighting and if there are viable solutions to stop the fighting ."

One of the civilian men in the group looked at the military men and said, "I think it is a power struggle between the generals, and unless one of the generals wins, there will not be peace!" He elaborated his point, "Some of the leaders of the opposition move- ments, such as General Mohamed Aydid and Colonel Abdillahi Yusuf and General Mohamed Siad Barre, started their military career together as corporals. For years, they moved together up the ladder in the military rank until they all became generals and colonels. I think the generals and colonels who are leading the opposition militia are jealous of Siad Barre. They are saying to themselves, 'If Afweyne[17] did it and become a president, we can also do it and rule the country!"

Another civilian in the group seconded him, "I agree! They do not worry about their people and the country. A genuine nation- alist who loves his country does not employ only his clan to 'save a nation.' Each one of the militia leaders fighting the government is supported only by his tribe. They were all evil, power-seekers!" A former diplomat, Sharif, agreed with them by saying, "We are witnessing the fighting of the major Somali clans, led by clan generals and colonels. I think the solution to the conflict   resides with the titled clan leaders."

Another laughed and joked, "Have you forgotten that the Revolution buried tribalism and the titled leaders together in 1970? If we are lucky, we may find the skeleton of some who escaped the burial and dead in the desert!"

I said, "I think one way out of the crisis would be to arrange a meeting for the fighting parties and force them to negotiate." I paused for a moment, and I added, "I think the scheme of some of the diplomatic community to remove the President from power is counterproductive and is not in the interest of the So-mali people. It would create a power vacuum, and it would be impossible to fill in the future."

Ambassador Sharif agreed, "The diplomatic commu-nity needs to find out the agenda of the opposition groups. Especially, it must find out what the intentions of USC since it is the dominant fighting force in Mo-gadishu." Then he looked at the military men from the Hawiye clan, and added, "It is true that the policy of some of the foreign countries is to remove the present from the power which is counterproductive, and it is not in the interest of our country."

Colonel Mohamed added his concern, "I worry about the future. Given the opposition's lack of unity and agenda and the weakening position of the regime, it seems the country is heading to disaster."

I believed there were opportunities to avert the im-pending disaster. A settlement was possible if ambition did not blind the op- position leaders who were focused only on gaining the power, and the President responded confidently to the changing times. The energy of the diplomatic community and the Somali elders needed to aim at bringing together the warring parties for negoti-ation. I thought all significant stakeholders were obliged to stop siding with the regime or the opposition groups before it was too late. I think the military government, which controlled the life of the nation for decades, and the intellectuals who remained complacent were responsible for the nation's demise.

At the final stage of the conflict, some key people in the regime attached their future to the regime's fate and blindly supported the government. Unfortunately, these people did not believe they could shape their destiny and the destiny of the nation without the regime. I wondered who was obligated to whom, the people to the generals, or the generals to the people. On the other hand, little did we realize that the most significant perils of the nation were USC leader Aydid who was not only planning to fight the regime but also major Somali clans.

I left the general thinking of the many actors in Somali politics. Most of the Somali leaders had been educated abroad, and they came back with the values and culture of their host countries. Those who trained in the Arab world, like Mr. Mohamed, desired the solution for the Somali problem to come from the Arab countries. Those educated in the Western and communist countries yearn what their masters would like to see. They reminded me of Frantz Fanon's cry, 'The Black Faces, The White Masks.'18 I was not sure whether Somalis deserve a state.

After walking for a while, I came across a commotion not far from the general's house. A group of people was assembled at the gate of the North Korea Embassy. I thought looting was in progress, and the people were waiting for their turn to take what the armed looters leave behind in the building. But what was happening in the building was more sinister than an act of loot- ing.

Gangs were holding male diplomats on the upper floor of the building, and another group was raping the female on the ground floor. The people watching the attack said that the robbers were marauding armed gangs. I was shocked and ashamed of being a Somali. It dawned on me that it would take generations for Somalia to regain the respect of the world. I continued my walk home with a heavy heart and was startled occasionally by the explosions coming from downtown fighting

January 11, 1991
Mogadishu, Somalia

Do not Bury Dead Enemy

Today in the morning, I decided to visit my brother-in-law Jama, and his family, who lived in the Karaan neighborhood. There was no public transport, and I had no car. The few speed- ing vehicles in the streets belonged to the warring parties. The only way to get to the home of Jama was to walk.

I took Sinai road, where heavy fighting took place earlier in the week. It was quiet, and the battlefront moved around Villa Somalia and Daynile neighborhood. I arrived at the Peking Hotel after a long walk. The area was lifeless, but the magnitude of the destruction caused by the fight was staggering. Most of the buildings in the area were damaged. Charred military equipment litered the streets, and the stench of decaying bodies of dead people and animals loaded the air. The few standing walls ex- posed gaping holes left by the bullets and rock-ets. I continued my walk, accompanied by the occasional sound of an explosion from the fighting in Daynile area. Strayed bullets coming from afar occasionally dropped around me like a dry leaf, making a hushing sound.

The further I walked to Jama's house; the dropping of the strayed bullets increased. I quickly retreated to alleys running parallel to the main road. When I arrived at Peking Hotel, I was shocked. Dead bodies were piled at the crossroads to block the flow of the traffic. I continued my walk, and not far from the first pile of dead bodies, another heap of bodies blocked the main Sinai intersection. It was clear the USC militia buried along the streets their dead and took their wounded, but piled the regime, dead soldiers, to block the streets. It was apparent the govern- ment forces were unable to collect their dead and wounded. Sadly, the right of the dead to be buried with respect was violated.

There were few other people on the road and in the alleys. They dashed in both directions along the streets and took cover when they hear a hissing sound of bullet or thud of a shell. They were risking their lives to find their relatives who lived in the area, or they were checking their properties, which they abandoned earlier. It was painful to watch the horror and fright in the eyes of these innocent people. The further I traveled, the worse it became the carnage on the road. The piles of the dead bodies on the crossroads increased, and the stench of the burning debris and explosives became unbearable.

After I witnessed the destruction and devastation caused by the fight and heard the sound of the combat for many days, I lost the sense of fear. I overcame the dread of dying, and I did not pay much attention to the danger I was facing. But today, after I witnessed the savagery and the hopelessness of the situation, I felt it was not wise to continue my trip for many more hours to see my brother-in-law. I decided to return home.

At midday, I arrived at my neighborhood mosque. I was delighted to see a friend and a long-time neighbor, Faisal. After prayed, we left the mosque together and sat on a rock near the perimeter wall of the African village. We exchanged the information we had about the fighting, and then he asked me if I had moved my family out of the city.

I said, "I have not yet."

He was a bit surprised and asked me, "What are you waiting for?"

With some reservations, I said, "I think the situation will re- turn normal. You do not think so?"

He frowned and said, "I do not think so! I think it will not be normal for a long time to come! I am leaving for Hargeisa in a few days."

I wanted to know what information he had, "Why you think it will not be normal for a long time to come?"

He said, "The of USC militia are brainwashed. They aim at driving the Darod clan out of Mogadishu. He added, "They be- lieve the Darod people are un-believers who came from a foreign place, and took the Hawiye land and oppressed them for generations. They believe in confiscating the Darod assets, property, and women as reparation for the crimes they committed for generations."

I could not believe what I was hearing. I said, "I do not think that is true. They know that the Darod people are Somali, and they intermarried and worked with the Hawiye people since the birth of the Somali nation. They pray in the same mosques shoulder-to-shoulder. Many of them have Darod imams who lead their prayers in their mosques."

He laughed loudly and said, "It is sad, but people be-lieve what they want to believe when they are in need. Imagine when a respected individual among his clan tells the poor and the illiterate young men of his tribe that they have the right to take the property and the beautiful women of the 'enemy' clans. That is what is happening, whether you want to believe it or not!" After a long pause, he looked at me and said, "Most of the USC fighters are from the bush, and they have never met a Darod people. On the other hand, the Hawiye elite has a plan, and they are using the 'rural boys' to drive non-Hawiye out of Mogadishu."

I joked, "It is strange! The Banadiri[21] people of Mo-gadishu be- lieve that the people of the 'long fingers,' in-cluding the Hawiye, are foreigners who invaded and occupied their Banadiri land! I think they are right, be-cause the region is called Banadir, and it must belong to them. Maybe we are all invaders!"

I left Faisal, refusing to believe everything he said. I could not understand why he wanted to scare me to leave the city. How- ever, in hindsight, I thought there was an element of truth in what he was saying. I heard in the past that some Hawiye people be- lieve the Darod people came by boat and settled in Hawiye land. The Abgal, a sub-clan of Hawiye, they the following myth.

> "Hey Darod
> You may swim across the ocean,
> Or take a boat to your home,
> You (must) leave my land."

In the afternoon, the clouds covered the sky, and the weather was warm. I decided to visit my Egyptian friend, and when I arrived at his place, he took me to his living room. As usual, there were several senior Somali officials sipping tea. Most of them were men whom the president flushed out in the past, and it seemed they were positioning themselves to be included in the envisioned new regime. They were members of Hawiye, Darod, Rahanweyn, and another small Somali clan. There were no Isaq clan members among them. The prevailing public perception was that foreign governments that had vested interest in Somalia politics, especially Egypt, Italy, and the U.S., would take part in the formation of the forthcoming government. The people visiting the general and other foreign embassies were appealing to be included in the anticipated Somali administration.

Some of the men were members of the Manifesto group, and they carried a message to pass to the general. I suspected they wanted the general to convey their message to his government and the other Arab governments. We drank tea and exchanged the information we had on the fighting, and finally, the general asked if we had suggestions for stopping the fight.

I did not like the way he addressed us. It was as though we were students, and he was checking an assignment that he gave earlier. I declined to participate in the discussion and asked to be excused to leave, but the general urged me to stay, and a pointless discussion ensued. From what the men were predicting, it was clear the end of the regime was imminent. It was also apparent that the polarization of Somali clans with USC and Darod clans was almost complete. Then, one of the men raised his voice and began describing what sounded like a Manifesto group message.

He said, "The Manifesto committee wants the Egyptian Govern- ment and the Organization of Arab League to intervene in the So- mali fighting and help us find a solution for the conflict...." The man served as a Somali ambassador to many countries and was believed to be an experienced diplomat. He concluded his talk with what he thought was the root cause of the Somali conflict by saying, " Ethiopian and Kenya governments have agreed to partition Somalia." He added, "The Somali Arab Brothers, the Arab League, and the Muslim countries are obliged to counter this conspiracy and help us defend our country."

I found the analysis of the ambassador absurd and amusing. It was not clear whether the ambassador was delivering a Manifesto message or giving his opinion. It was true that Ethiopia and Kenya were involved in the destabilization of Somalia. It was also true that the opposition militias fighting the regime were trained and armed by Ethiopia and to some extent, supported by Kenya. But to blame the neighboring countries for our lack of common sense, and the upheaval and self-destruction was a gross exaggeration. Without doubt, bad governance, corruption, nepotism, and injustice committed by the regime, and the misguided ambition of the opposition movements were the root causes of Somali conflict. Furthermore, the grievances of the USC and other militias fighting the regime could not justify by the devastation they incurred. They were replacing the rule of law with clan anarchy, destruction, slaughter, and expulsion of the innocent population from their homes, which could not be explained by any measure. Sadly, the Somali elite was looking for the root cause of the problem of their nation everywhere except themselves. Maybe it would have been easier to find the answer to the problems of the country if they pause for a moment and they search their souls. They blamed others for their plight and looked in the wrong places for the solution. It seemed the Somali people developed the habit of expecting an external power to arrive at zero hours and save them from annihilation. It seemed the concept of the rule of law was alien to them.

Before the general could respond, the door of the room plunged open, and a crying Iraqi ambassador and his family rushed. The general jumped to his feet to and received them. The sobbing women and children rushed back into the kitchen area. The ambassador continuously lamented, "They looted my embassy, and almost raped my wife and children!" He added that the embassy drivers and some of the Somali embassy employees saved them.

He continued his shocking tale in a despairing voice, repeating the word 'loss' in Arabic. The general took the ambassador to a corner and comforted him. They kept whispering for a long time. It was apparent they were talking about a safe exit to their countries. I wondered why Sadam Hussein abandoned the symbol of Iraq in Somalia. I thought maybe Somalia was not alone in the camp of the states ruled by the whim of dictators.

I left the group without good news to my mother. On my way home, I came across looting in progress at the 'Casa-Populare' branch of the Somali Commercial bank. The looters were gangs who supported the USC and other militia groups, as the signs on their clothes displayed. They bored holes on the front wall of the bank and entered and came out with bags of paper money. The women, children, and the elderly were waited outside beside the building and fought over what dropped from the bags the strong

looters brought out of the bank. The government soldiers were watching the show from a nearby dugout at 'Primo-Lulio' area, and they occasionally fired in the direction of the bank. They probably had not received their salary for many months. But they did not dare to take part in the bonanza, even though they were carrying big guns.

January 12, 1991
Mogadishu, Somalia

Settling Scores

On the morning of January 12, I decide to visit my younger brother, who moved earlier his family to his workshop in Medina district. I took the road near the Digfer Hospital that runs through the Medina District. I arrived at the Ministry of Foreign Affairs momentarily and was shocked by the staggering destruction. The public and private properties in the area were vandalized with a vengeance that defied belief. They completely ransacked all the government ministries and agencies in the area. The most affected institutions were the Ministries of Higher Education, Foreign Affairs, Planning, and the National Water Agency. Government documents, shattered furniture, and broken office equipment covered the grounds of the buildings, the neighboring alleys, and the surrounding grounds of the areas.

The Ministry of Foreign Affairs sustained the most savage as- sault. Thousands of documents, including passport booklets, covered its grounds. The secrets of the state, collected over decades, including documents dealing with the Somali affairs of neighbor- ing countries of Ethiopia and Kenya, were scattered everywhere. The documents were there on the ground to be read or collected for everyone to see and collect if they want, including the enemies of the Somali people. It appeared the looters took what they could use or sell and shredded the rest. A broken piano with a missing leg was lying on its side in the middle of the main street, and a small boy crawled under it and was try-ing to play it. An onlooker shouted, "The piano fell from the office of the minister." It seemed the looters thought the government institutions were a part of the tools the regime used to oppress them.

I continued my walk toward the Banadir Hospital. Many dead bodies were scattered in the street parallel to the wall of the hospital. A wounded man leaning on the hospital wall was begging for help. He was unable to move his shattered legs. Shockingly, the people passed him hurriedly, ignoring his desperate plea for help. The sight of a dying man at the gate of the hospital, not get-ting help from his people, was sickening. We could carry him in- side the hospital to save him. However, maybe we thought he was fortunate to die quickly than wait for the imminent end of his life if not by a bullet, for sure, by starvation. Perhaps, we were saying to ourselves, 'let him go immediately to escape the un- known future and the trauma engulfing the living!' Perhaps, we thought he would not receive the help he needs if he is not from the 'chosen clan.' Maybe, those us not heeding to his plea be-lieved that we would not live much longer after him. Perhaps we did not understand the difference between the living and the dead anymore.

The wounded man and the dead people in the street were from the Abgal clan. They were attacked and killed by men from Gal- gala Abgal sub-clan, who held animosity to other Abgal sub- clans. The Galgala people claimed that they migrated from the Majeerteen area in the north of the country a long time ago, and they settled in the Abgal area near the Banadir region. The Abgal clan adopted them, but they were scorned and oppressed and considered outcast. After they endured humiliation and discrimination for being outsiders for many years, they declared their ancestors and announced that they belong to the Majerrteen clan. The Galgala armed men ambushed the fleeing Hawiye people, especially the Abgal, at the intersection of Banadir Hospital. It was payback time – and the law of the jungle, the Somali style was in full swing.

I continued walking with a quick pace toward Medina to reach the factory of my brother. We decided to bring my mother to his place and assembled armed relatives and truck and went back to my house. We picked my mother and sister and drove back to the workshop without incident.

The workshop had a large hall, a small office, and a toilet. The hall contained several machines with different sizes. The family of my brother was already there. We divided the hall into several sections between and around the machines. One corner, we assigned to the women (my mother, my sister, my sister-in-law, and other females), and the children. Other corners we allocated to the men and the two remaining corners on the sides of the door, we decided to be a kitchen and a toilet.

There was no regard for Somali and Islam customs, which put a barrier between women and men. Sisters-in-law, and brothers- in-law slept in the same hall without privacy. The workshop was not suitable for habitation since its floor was covered with pieces of wood, nails, glue, and a lot of other construction materials that were dangerous to both the children and grown-ups. It was not a place for children to live and play. We had no idea how long we were staying there, or how long it would be safe. Nevertheless, no one complained, and we just prayed for our ordeal to end. Armed young men brought us guns and ammunition, and they stayed with us.

The fighting continued, and it spread in most areas of the city. The USC militia, and its supporters, and unknown and menacing gangs controlled most of the city. Only a few pockets, including Villa Somalia and some areas in Daynile, the seaport, the airport, and some area in the Medina District, remained under the control of the regime. On the other hand, some neighborhoods, such as Mecca Mukarama Street, Afasiyoni encampment, and Industrial Road, the situation was fluid and were not controlled by both sides. Most of the government forces had either defected and joined their respective clans or withdrew to their camps and assumed defensive positions.

What remained of the government troops that continued to defend the regime were from the Darod clan or people aged in the army or in other security forces. The killing on both warring sides and on the innocent civilians caught in the crossfire or in- tentionally killed for being from undesired clans by USC militia or regime soldiers continued to grow exponentially. The destruction of property was beyond comprehension, and most of the downtown buildings and the celebrated landmarks were obliterated beyond recognition. The looters continued to raid businesses and burn them after emptying their contents.

The division of the city into clan-controlled enclaves led to the displacement of a large number of people who were trying to reach areas controlled by their clans. The people who stayed out of their clan areas encountered horrifying ordeals, and in most times, lived without food and water. The displaced people included government officials who lost their privileges and protection because of the conflict. Most of them came to Medina District and moved into unoccupied and abandoned homes.

The senior government officials were forced to taste the low life of the dis-advantaged, laborers, and the outcast. They never imagined the probability of living among the majority of the population who lived in appalling conditions. Instead of sleeping in air-conditioned homes, they were forced to lay their backs on a cold, dirty floor without soft mattresses, feather pillows, and sheets with soothing scents. The cherished women of the elite of the nation who visited Europe and Arab capitals for shopping were forced to sleep in a crowded spaces full of flies and undesirable people. The esteemed few ladies who had no responsibility besides beautifying themselves were forced to share an open latrine full of cockroaches, maggots, and fly, with their former bodyguards, and house servants who used to massage their feet.

The elite, who dined with prime lamb ribs, when most people slept with empty stomachs, were forced to eat white rice, cooked in barrel with dirty water. Only hard and muddy water from open wells was available to wash down the dry and flavorless rice instead of beer, cold soda, or juice. It was a dreadful situation nobody envisioned or wanted to happen.

Unfortunately, the militia group leaders were not different from the leaders of the regime they were fighting to unseat. Their attitude was different from an incident I heard about a military coup in an African country which occurred in 1961. The coup leaders of that country took hostage the rich ministers and the essential people of the regime and placed them in a military hangar. They fed them with leftovers collected from the city dumpsters for several days to show them what the poor people of their country ate to survive. The leaders of Somali opposition movements could not be compared with these African coup leaders of 1961. The generals leading the USC, SSDF, SPM, and SNM were sociopaths, who misled their innocent clans to gain power. They were hypocrites who told their clans that they wound feed them honey and milk when they take power on their behalf.

At noon, Radio Mogadishu unexpectedly came on air, after it had been silent for many days. It announced a peace proposal tabled by the Italian government to the Somali president. It contained several important points, including a suggestion for the president to relinquish most of his powers, but to stay in power. It also contained a request for forming a new cabinet, including all the warring parties. It surprising that a foreign government to tell the president of a nation to surrender power. No wonder, many Somalis believed the international community sided the opposition groups and was deter-

mined to remove the president from power. It was rumored that only Italy and Egypt were will- ing to keep
the president in power until a party in the conflict
emerges as a winner.

During my employment at the Ministry of Information as di- rector of Radio Mogadishu and Managing Director of Somali Broadcasting Service, and later as the
Director of Somali National Television, I met many
diplomats from different countries. Some of them held
mysterious jobs in their embassies, but they were hiding
under the diplomatic umbrella. Our meetings were official and related to business. Usually, they visited the
ministry of in- formation when they needed public an-
nouncements for visiting delegations from their countries and when they want to broadcast documentaries of
anniversaries of their nations, such as their in- dependence days or documentaries. In these meetings, we had
extensive discussions, and some of them talked openly
about sensitive matters related to Somali affairs. Sometimes displayed an aversion towards the Somali regime
and its president. At times, they wanted to know my
views regarding the Somali regime policies, Western
countries, and the Somali president, and they also mentioned other senior officials. They sometimes mentioned
the names of people they thought were corrupt. I always
reminded them that I was not a politician and unaware
of the issues they were talking about. However, for some
of them who were persistent, I told that the Somali people preferred corrupt country- men than the foreigners
who believed that their dogs were more intelligent than
the natives.

Some of the diplomats I met were disappointed

when I refused to agree with their viewpoints. I remember a U.S. diplomat who believed that some Somali clans were colonizing other Somali clans. I also recall one of the first secretaries of the Italian Embassy, who knew very little about Somali society and history, and talked as though Somalia was still under Italian rule. He was not listening to what I was saying but just lectured me on how he wanted Somalia to be governed. Maybe that was how his govern- ment wanted Somalia to be run.

The ridicule of some diplomats toward the Somali leaders was profound, and I suspected their views were a reflection of the content of the Somali country files in their foreign ministries. Most of them had a foggy idea about Somali thinking, and as a result, their contacts with Somali opposition groups and the So- mali regime could produce for them a clear understanding of So- mali politics. It was clear that their main concern was only to safeguard their national interests. It was a known fact that foreign countries were providing the Somali oppositions moral and material support without giving much thought to the impact of these supports on the Somali sovereignty. In particular, Many Somalis believed that the United States policy was driven by anger and focused on retaliating the humiliation Siad Barre caused the United States when he expelled it from Somalia in the early 1970s when it got a better deal from the Soviet Union. When the Cold War ended and the Soviet Union collapsed, Somalia lost its strategic importance, and as a result, the West led by the .U.S. lost interest and abandoned Somalia. It was obvious that most foreign diplomats came to Somalia with a negative view of the country.

In addition to the scientific socialism that Somalia upheld, the international community regarded Somalia as a place of hard- ship. The developed countries sent only entry-level diplomats with little or no experience. Most of them, especially those from developing countries, had almost nothing to do during their assignment in Somalia. The diplomats from developed countries were in the country only to restrict the influence of their adversaries, and they had limited contact with the Somali public. They attended only a few of the Somali national anniversaries, such as Somali Independence Day and some religious celebrations. As a sign of friendship, some embassies held receptions on their national holidays and invited Somali government officials and prominent civil society members, and the government mass media attended most of these functions. The embassies served plenty of food and alcohol, and some Somalis guests drank alcohol like camel milk since it was not available on the market. Be- sides these rare contacts, the international community members were counting the number of days remaining for them to stay in the country. Most of the Arab and Muslim diplomats were enjoying the freedom of drinking alcohol and entertaining each other in their fortified homes and embassy compounds. Only the Saudi Arabia Embassy projected a public religious image and some- times distributed the Holy Book (the Koran).

After both the West and socialist/communist countries lost interest in Somalia, I wondered if they had anything for Somalia except removing its president from power? On numerous occasions, I asked some of the diplomats I met what they would like to see if the regime is changed. They always gave elusive re- sponses, although many of them knew very little of Somali politics, history, and culture and had no interest in Somali future. They talked as though they knew what was right for Somalia more than the Somalis themselves. From their attitude, one could infer that they held the old white man's belief of Africans being uncivilized, and butcher each other when they could not find white people to the slaughter. They believed the Africans to be backward, uncivilized, and unable to govern themselves. Some diplomats behaved as the colonial masters and wanted the Somali regime to adhere to the directives of their former colonial masters, and if they deviate from it to expect the help, they were receiving to be terminated.

Unexpectedly, late in the afternoon, Radio Mogadishu came on-air and announced the appointment of a presidential commit- tee. However, many people were interested or believed or trusted the effectiveness of the new community. and on the other had the USC leadership, especially General Aydid was not interested in the olive branch of the regimes

January 13, 1991
Mogadishu, Somalia

The Killing Fields of Mogadishu

It was almost two weeks since the fighting erupted between the USC militia and the Siyad Barre regime in Mogadishu. This day, before the morning prayer, the USC movement attempted to overrun the defenses of Villa Somalia, where the resident hangs on power. The USC was severely beaten back on its earlier attempt to overwhelm Villa Somalia. It sustained substantial losses, and because of the setback, it weakened the Hawiye unity and also dented the USC confidence. Earlier, the USC militia split into two factions, and the one led by general Aydid, which got most of its support from the Habargidir clan of Hawiye tribe, was determined to continue to fight to the end despite the setback at the Villa Somalia. But none Habrgidir clan leaders of Hawiye clans, including Abgal, Murursade, and others. began to contemplate to withdrew from the campaign.

The situation became worrisome when two Libyan warships arrived at the Mogadishu seaport, which was controlled at the time by the regime forces. A Rumor circulated that the ships were carrying arms for the regime, and it shook the confidence of the wavering Hawiye clans. However, the content of the vessels was a part of a previous arrangement between the two countries. The USC followers believed that the Government would use the arms to crush their uprising, and it would deny them to oust the dying regime. As a result, the USC leaders formed a Hawiye committee of elders to shore up the unity of Hawiye clans. The new commit- tee, after extensive meetings, it restored the unity of the tribe, and the wavering groups agreed to continue the struggle.

Both warring sides, the USC, and the regime spread wild rumor to win the public support. One of the misinformation rumors spread by the USC militia stated that the Somali 2nd Vice President, Hussein Kulmiye Afrah, has defected and took refuge in the Italian embassy. Another rumor asserted that Mohamed Ibrahim Egal, one of Somali former Prime Ministers, who only a few months earlier circulated an open letter analyzing the politi- cal situation of the Somali state to the foreign embassies in Mogadishu was conferring with foreign diplomats. Many people wondered and said if some of the Somali leaders took refuge in foreign embassies. And others were counseling foreign diplomats, and it seemed no one was working for the Somali people.

The regime began to retreat from some of the positions it held in the front lines, and the USC militia quickly replaced them and continued to pressure the regime forces. As the conflict dragged on, the fleeing of prominent government officials out of Mogadishu increased. The exodus included cabinet ministers, political party members, senior military leaders, and middle and lower government employees. To stop this human out follow, the President created a Crisis Management Committee. The commit- tee members included President himself, General Abdulqadir Haji Mohamed, a close relative of the President, whose father helped the President when he was orphaned. Other   committee members were General Ahmed Suleiman Abdulla, the son-in-law of the President, and General Mohamed Ali Samatar, the 1st Vice President since 1969, and General Mohamed Said Hirsi Morgan, another son-in-law of the President.

The second vice president, Hussein Kulmiye Afrah, from the Hawiye tribe, was not included in the committee. The absence of the second vice president was an indication that the President was not trusting a Hawiye, even a member of the Central Committee (SRC) that ruled the country for more than 20 years. The President lost the support of most Somali people except his family and clan. He could not even count on the loyalty of the tested few, who had been faithful to him for decades. The people on the new committee were family members and a few individuals who believed they would not have a future if the President removed from power and were forced to hang with him to the end. The people familiar with Somali politics believed that the President was out of options, and the committee he named was just another futile attempt to stay in power that continued to crumble under his feet.

By this day, the collapse of the Somali state was apparent. Feu- dal-fief like mini-clan enclaves, vying for power appeared all over the city. The state symbols, including the blue flag with the white star dear to all Somalis, disappeared overnight. They replaced with clan names - Daron, Hailey,

Isaq, or Rahanweyn. The for- mer Somali politicians and
diplomats, who represented the So- mali state in the country, abroad and dined with world leaders, were forced to
stoop to form clan committees and conferred with clan
scoundrels. The feared and respected Somali national army
generals and colonels lowered themselves to recruit, lead,
and in- cited wild and uncultured clan militia to attack other
clans. The members of minority clans and the vulnerable
members of the population- mothers, and children, who lost
everything they had unfortunately sought help from the
committees of warring major tribes.

Today, at midday prayer, I met a friend named   Abdulqadir, who worked at the film Agency of the Ministry
of Information. He was from the Majerteen clan and a
member SSDF opposition movement. When the fighting
started, he moved with other friends into an abandoned
building in the suburb of the city, near Abdi Hosh compound. The several floor buildings belonged to the former Somali Prime Minister, Mohamed Ibrahim Egal. Mr.
Abdulqadir printed flyers and other propaganda material that supported the SSDF movement and its fight
against the regime. He also glorified USC successes and
approved its relationship with the SSDF militia.

He invited me to his new place to have tea. We entered an empty living room with solar-powered radio
communication equipment, printers, and duplicators.
The speakers of the communication radio were blar-
ing incomprehensible messages that were probably
coming from SSDF militia people. He tried to respond, but the transmission was so bad that he became frustrated and started cursing the radio and the
people at the other end. The copies of discarded flyers

that congratulated USC for the victories it scored and its cooperation with SSDF littered the floor of the room. The place was dirty, and the heat of the month January turned it into an uncomfortable and stinking hole. He looked me with inquiring eyes and said, "What have you heard about the fighting?"

I shrugged and said, "I haven't heard much, and I don't know what the future holds. But I worry!"

He tried to comfort me. "I talked with some Somalis who work for foreign embassies, and they told me that the situation would get better soon."

It seemed Somalis were waiting for the foreigners to solve their problems. It seemed my friend was ill-informed or unaware that the USC was ravaging the city, and thousands of people were being killed or fleeing the city daily. I said, "The regime has al- ready exhausted its energy, and It cannot force the opposition to accept a negotiated settlement. The opposition, especially USC, has no political agenda and exit strategy. It is obsessed with the ousting the regime and taking power, at any price. And in the process, the prevailing anarchy and clan politics is destroying our country. I am sure you have heard the disintegration of our arm forces and that its members are joining the fighting with their respective clans and inciting revenge." I added, "All sides are resorting to 'tribalizing' the conflict, and if the fighting continues in the present state, it will consume the nation, and no one would emerge the victor! " I pondered for a moment and then continued, "The opposition movements have no idea of what it takes to form a government and running a state!"

He agreed and said, "I think the opposition realizes the seriousness of the situation, and it knows that it will not be easy to remove the president from the power."

The conflict spread to the rest of the country, and the security in the regions rapidly deteriorated. After the army, the police, and other security organs melted away days after the conflict erupted in Mogadishu, the members of the arm forces took all the armaments, including artillery pieces, tanks and more, and joined their respective clans. In every region, clan-based militias began to fight for control of state property and confiscating state assets. When the fighting started in Mogadishu, in addition to USC, the other opposition militias – the SSDF, SNM, and SPM,   which fought the regime launched operations in their respective clan areas. The SNM infiltrated Hargeisa and Burao, the capital cities of Northwest and Together, and they took control of the govern- ment institutions. They removed all government symbols and expelled all none-Isaq government employees. The SNM militia used force against Darod people and communities and forced them to flee to Ethiopia, southern Somalia, and the Sool, Sanag and Ayn regions.

On the other hand, in the same period, the SPM movement caused havoc in Jubaland and abused the none-Absame clans, including members of some of the Darod clans suspected of sup- porting the regime. In Central Somalia, the SSDF moved into the Majeerteen areas and began forming local administrations. It also sent some of its forces and militia leaders to Mogadishu.

I turned again to Abdulqadir, who was busy duplicating a flyer. I asked what he had heard about the conflict. He only answered my question with a question,

"Why the Darod clan is not united? Do we know what the Isaq clan is doing in the North?"

To boost his ego and his hopes for SSDF and USC anticipated victory, I said, "Most of the Darod clans are united, and they are not supporting the regime. As you may know, some of the Darod clans waged war against the regime for many years. These clans, especially the

Majerteen and Ogaden clans believed they suffered greatly, and they are determined to oust the regime."

My answer did not excite Abdilqadir. He suspected that I did not believe what I was saying. But even then, he wanted to hear more, "Do we know the position of the SNM?" He asked.

I was sure he knew what was happening in the Isaq area, especially in the major cities and towns. I said, "The Isaq clan has suffered considerably under the regime, and its SNM movement has allied with USC and the Ogaden-based SPM against the regime. I suspect the Isaq clan is confronting the regime support- ers in its area."

His blank gazes suggested his awareness of the SNM move- ment activities. He was aware of the dilemma his movement, the Majeerteen-based SSDF, was facing. The Majerteen SSDF was in a catch-22 situation. Although it had opposed and engaged in armed struggle against the regime since 1978, It now faced the fury of USC-Aydid function with the rest of the Darod civilian population. It also needed to resolve its internal conflict before it takes a meaningful role in the continually changing conflict. Its previous alliance with the USC, SNM, and SPM opposition move- ments ended when the USC-Aydid function anti-Darod rhetoric made most Majerteen SSDF militia fighters want to abandon the struggle to oust the

regime. The weakening of its alliance with other opposition movements and the lack of unifying leadership
(Colonel Abdillahi Yusuf, the leader and founder of
SSDF was not released from Ethiopian Jail yet) raised the
possibility of the movement joining the forces defending
the Siyad Barre regime.

On the other hand, as mentioned earlier, the USC
movement split into several functions, and the group
led by jointly prominent Hawiye elders wanted a negotiated settlement to save the city from destruction.
Another anti-Darod function led by Aydid sniffed victory and pumped its chest like an angry gorilla and
was intent on fighting on and removing the regime
from the power. Furthermore, as a policy, the USC
movement reneged from its alliance with the Darod
opposition movements of the SSDF and SPM. It was
only appreciating the congratulations coming from
the SNM movement and supporters.

The Darod front unity was in disarray – my friend
Mr. Abdulqadir believed his Majerteen clan was facing
numerous   internal critical challenges. One hand, a
prominent Majerteen general, Mohamed Said Hirsi (
AKA) Morgan, the son-in-law of the President, and a
diehard supporter wanted his clan to support the
regime. He assembled a formidable militia from his clan
at the National Stadium to support his father-in-law. On
the other hand, the SSDF supporters in Nairobi and the
SSDF military wing commander, Colonel Gadhdhere,
adamantly rejected the idea of de- fending the regime
they fought for many years to unseat. Unfortunately, the
man who could unify the clan and lead the movement
and give a direction, Colonel Abdillahi Yusuf, was still

in an Ethiopian jail, and as a result, the movement lacked military and political leadership.

Even though the Majerteen clan was the first to start the Somali opposition movements, the SSDF in Ethiopia and waged war for many years, it began to lose steam because of several factors, including economic and leadership. Throughout its struggle, the SSDF movement did not only targeted the security forces of the regime, but it also attacked some of the Darod clans, in particular, the clan of the President Marehan and the Dhulbahante clan which was one of the allies of Marehan. These actions alienated the clan and made it renegade among most of the other Darod clans.

Starting from its inception in1978, the SSDF blamed the regime for the collective punishment of its tribe. It accused the Govern- ment of killing the Majerteen people without impunity, demolishing their boreholes and reservoirs, allowing soldiers to rape its women, and massacred their livestock to starve the people to subdue them. The SSDF accused the regime of jailing its prominent members without due process. These allegations carried sufficient truth.

After the establishment of the SSDF and other opposition movements in Ethiopia, clashes between the Somali Army and the Ethiopia-supported movements on the provisional border be- tween the two countries became frequent and sometimes deadly. The opposition movements also regularly attacked the towns and villages of the clans deemed to support the regime. For instance the SSDF attacked and looted the main town of Dhulbahante Buuhoodle several times.

The Somali Government informed the international

community of the encounters at the border and blamed Ethiopia of aggression on its territory. In particular, the Somali Government informed the United States government and asked for help. Un- fortunately, the Somali Government was unable to prove the Ethiopian incursion into its territory. Then in mid-July 1982, a combined force of SSDF and Ethiopian military units captured medium-size Somalia towns of Galdogob and Balanbale. Galdogob was about 60 km from the capital of Mudug province Galkayo, and it is located on the Somali side of the provisional borderline19. The occupying force was heavily armed with armored vehicles and tanks, which was not typical for a clan militia. After the Somali national army was forced to withdraw from the town, the inhabitants fled, and the occupying forces looted the town.

The occupation of Galdogob and other Somali border towns and villages by the joint forces SSDF and Ethiopia alarmed the Somali regime. It suspected that Ethiopian was preparing to capture the central part of Somalia to split the country into two halves. The Ministry of Information and National Guidance sent a team to Galkayo to report on the fighting. I headed the team, and it included reporters from Radio Mogadishu, the October Star newspaper, the Somali National News Agency, and a cameraman and photographer from Somali Film Agency. We traveled in two vehicles and an OB van (Outside Broadcasting Van).

We arrived in Galkayo in the evening. The highway, which brought us to Galkayo, was built by the Chinese Government, and it ran through the city, dividing it into two sections. As we drove through the city, we noticed that the north side of the city was not lighted, and the south side was glowing with lights. The officials of the regime and the city received us and took us to a government guesthouse. We asked them, why half of the city is not lighted, and they proudly said, "The anti-regime elements and they blew the generator which supplied electricity. They thought they were hurting the Government." We understood that they meant "SSDF supporters populate the dark section of the   city."

The following morning, we visited the frontline, and the troops facing the enemy in Galdogob. The commanders allowed us to go as far as possible to the front line and take pictures and film what appeared to be 'combined forces of SSDF militia and Ethiopian military units.' We returned to the city and dispatched a life report to Radio Mogadishu from the OB van. Unfortunately, we could not see from afar anything that proofed to be the presence of an Ethiopian army.

The following day, early in the morning, twelve Ethiopian Mig 21 fighter jets raided the airport of the city, which housed a few Somali Mig 17 fighters. The twelve Ethiopian Mig fighters were in a tight formation of three squadrons of four planes each, and each one flew over the airport runway and dropped bombs. The airport old antiaircraft guns opened fire, to defend the airport from the attacking planes. Our cinematographer and photographer tried to capture an image of the enemy planes, but we were not sure of what we got. We decided to send the films to Mogadishu to be developed and waited for the result to come back to Galkayo.

The dropped bombs created huge craters on the runway. It was apparent the raid aimed at damaging the runway to prevent the few Somali Mig 17 fighters from taking off to bomb the Ethiopian forces on the border near Galdogob and Balanbale. We reported the incident to the Ministry Information in Mogadishu and also mentioned the existence of film and photos we thought we had.

A fact-finding American delegation arrived in the afternoon in Galkayo to inspect the airport raid and met military personnel and civilian officials. In the morning, the delegation visited the frontline and airport and examined the craters perforated by the Ethiopian bombs. My team gave them the negatives we assumed were containing the jets bombarding the airport, and the delegation returned to Mogadishu. The next day, we heard the negatives we gave to the American delegation contained no images. We were not surprised, and we knew our old cameras would not capture a picture or video of the supersonic Mig 21 fighters.

Another Darod clan, the Ogaden, also harbored regime animosity. It formed an Ogaden-based SPM opposition movement in Ethiopia and blamed the regime for crimes carried against its people in Jubbaland. It accused the state that it collectively punished its people by killing innocent people, raping women, and poisoning water wells to wipe out their livestock to subdue them. It also blamed the regime for unrelenting hostility and vindictive campaigns against the population of its cities and village. Thus, the SPM movement waged guerrilla attacks against government security forces and the clans supporting the regime for several years. At this time, the SPM militia led by colonel Ahmed Omar Jess with limited muscle was marching toward Mogadishu from Afgoe town to join USC-Aydid.

Another Darod sub-clan Dhulbahante, was caught in the conflict unprepared. Its leading politicians worked and supported the regime, and were not trusted by the other Darod sub-clans. A significant number of its members held important government posts for a long time, and two of its sons were the sons-in-law of the President. Many Somali people unfairly accused the whole clan of being spies for the regime. Furthermore, both Majeerteen and Absame, who were close relatives of Dhulbahante than the Marehan, accused them of betrayal for allying with their enemy the Marehan.

On top of all these Somali clan fragmentation and hostility, the USC movement succeeded in spreading negative propaganda, demonizing the Darod clan. It told its supporters that the previous Somali regimes were always formed only from the Darod clan, and the Hawiye clan and other none-Darod clans were denied their rights and were oppressed by the Darod regimes. The USC movement urged the Hawiye tribe to take back what was rightfully theirs – the land and the Government. As a result, in Mogadishu, the USC removed all Darod government employees from their positions and replaced them with USC clan members. Instead of uniting the Somali people who suffered equally under the military regime, irrespective of their clan affiliation, and launch a new era of hope and prosperity, the USC leaders, betrayed its alliance of the Darod opposition movements of SSDF and SPM and began to target all Darod people in the hope of establishing a Somalia state governed only by Hawiye clan. The USC movement mistakenly believed that after the 'liberation' Mogadishu, the rest of the country would follow and will fall in place.

I left Abdulqadir with mixed feelings. I decided to check my apartment at the African village where we left our possessions. The USC militia had come close to the African village area, and the Labor Road was now the dividing line between the two war- ring parties. When I arrived at the Hotel Taleh area[20], I entered the edge of the fighting. The regime soldiers and supporters were holding a position in and around Hotel Taleh, and the USC militia was firing from behind the retaining wall of the National Fair Ground. I continued at a brisk pace from the Banadir Secondary School area, ducking behind the walls of buildings. Unexpectedly, a man in a ragged military uniform jumped out of a bush and pointed a gun at me. I was shocked and froze in my heels, and my dry throat produced an unintelligible utterance. He planted the barrel of his gun hard on my chest and demanded, "Who are you? (Ayaad tahay?)"

I said in a quavering voice, "I am Somali."

He thrust the barrel of the gun to my throat and shouted again, "Fuck Somalia and your fuck your mom! Who are you? I am not asking you again!"

I knew I could not reason with him or tell him to remove the uniform he was given to protect me. Before I could tell him my clan, which was the 'ID' he was asking, which might also cost my life, another man emerged from a nearby shade and told him to let me go. The second man, I presumed, knew me or perhaps was against the war.

I ran toward 1st July Square. I then took the alley behind Horsed officers Club to reach my apartment. The ally ran through an area covered with bushes and sand dunes. I came across a shocking and repulsive sight. The area was 'a killing field.' Human corpses covered the ground, and from the state of their decay of the bodies, it was clear they were killed at different times. Some of the bodies were covered with blood, and a brown liquid dripped from them. Other bodies were swollen and ready to burst, and some other bodies exposed broken bones, held together by a brittle and baked skin. A swarm of flies feasted on the bodies, and the ground under them was soaked with drainage. Multitude maggots crawled over each other on the bodies, searching for a soggy dark spot to hide from the scourging sun. The stench of the decomposing bodies was intolerable and covered my face with the sleeve of my shirt. The toiling maggots, fighting for their lives, captured my imagination. I asked myself if they were different from the unarmed and innocent civilians fleeing for their lives.

I finally arrived at my apartment. The looters ransacked it, and the furniture and fixtures were gone. Even the wires in the walls were ripped off. The floor was littered with broken glasses and ruined household items. Only the bare walls were still standing. I walked back to my new place in the Medina district, thinking about the dark future the nation faces, and I feared and worried for my family. It dawned on me the immense task awaiting the future generations. Who would bear the responsibility of rescuing the nation to be called a state again? For sure, history would not be kind to those who misled their clans, stamped out Somali nationalism, and elevated 'clannism' to gain personal power.

January 14, 1991
Mogadishu, Somalia

A Death in the Family

The fighting was heavy in several areas for the last 24 hours. It was reported an indiscriminate bombing by the government forces on the USC-held neighborhoods. As rumored, the casualty of the fighting included the burning of the Sinai market to the ground and the spread of the heavy fighting to new areas, including the State Navy Headquarters.

Many people escaped from the combat zone and arrived in South side of the city, and they reported that the warring parties were abusing the civilian population. The government fighters suspected the civilians living in the combat areas to be a threat and supporters of the USC and harassed them to leave their homes, which was a clear indication of a human rights violation and a war crime. On the other hand, the fleeing civilians brought with them severe and horrifying atrocities committed by the USC militia. They reported widespread assaults done by the USC militia, which in many ways, could be considered to be worse than the human rights violations perpetrated by the government forces. They reported an indiscriminate raping, killing, and looting, carried mostly on the Darod civilians living in what became USC-controlled areas. Because of the fear of the USC militia's mis- conduct, many people fled North of the city and arrived in the southern town.

In hindsight, one could argue, the USC militia rejected the Darod opposition movements' position to save the Somali unity and form a united Somali front encompassing all Somali opposition movements to hasten the exit of the regime and its leader President Said Barre. The USC position forced some of the Darod opposition movements to fight the USC militia and defend the system that ruined their clans.

The intriguing question was why some ordinary folks were slaughtering members of opposition clans in the name of clan honor? The only obvious answer was that the leaders on both sides were exploiting the emotion of ordinary people in the name of a so-called defense of clan interest to achieve their malicious goal of gaining power. The warring parties were oblivious of the plight of their people and the hundreds who died under their feet. They were both willing to torch the city and the country to rise from its ashes as victorious.

Later in the day, I heard the most painful news since the conflict started. I was told my brother Abdi and his only son Hasan, my nephew Abdi'aziz Ismail (Dakhare), and my niece Amina Jama were all murdered by the USC militia. As a daily routine, my brother Abdi, my nephew Abdi'aziz, and their friend collected and buried the bodies of slain people from the street around the Sheikh Nur compound to bury them. When Hasan, who was not with his father at the time, heard the incident, he rushed to the Sheikh Nur compound where his father was killed to find out how his father died, and if possible, to retrieve his body for burial. Unfortunately, on his way, he was also captured by the USC militia and was killed too. We were unable to recover their bodies to give them a dignified Islamic burial.

It was just the other day when I visited my brother Abdi at Sheikh Nur compound. He was sitting with his son Hasan under a tree. We talked about whereabouts of the rest of the family and agreed that the situation in the city was getting dangerous, in particular in the Sheikh Nur area.

However, he philosophized the situation and said, "The Soma- lis are unthankful for the blessing that God bestowed upon them. They adopted the culture of the unbelievers and discarded the messages of Allah contained in the Holy Book. The scripture is a manual for man to follow during the short time he/she lives on this earth! Unfortunately, we brought upon ourselves the destruction we are facing now."

I did not want to argue with him or disagree with his conviction or philosophy, which focused on the Divine and serving others. However, I wanted him to understand that the Somali conflict had nothing to do with the religion. I told him that the conflict was turning into a war of Somali clans or civil war. I added that the regime was unable to enforce the laws of the land and failed to defend the Somali unity. I warned him that the Hawiye and Isaq clans are attacking the Darod clan everywhere, and that has nothing to do with religion! If you are from the Darod clan, they will kill you. You cannot hide from the USC militias and roaming gangs, and as you know, our family is not in this area to protect you!"

He gave me a strange look and said," No man can escape the will of Allah! As soon as the dictator Siad Barre relinquishes the power, things will return to normal, and all Somalis will reconcile and bury their hatchets. Meanwhile, the people will suffer, be- cause, in all conflicts, the ordinary man is always the   victim."

His son and I pleaded with him to join us, and we reminded him that the roaming gangs would not reason with him and surely would kill him. He rejected our plea and insisted on stay- ing and working for 'the next world.' He recited a verse from the Koran to reinforce his decision, "No one can delay or bring for- ward the hour of the departure of the soul from this world."

He blessed us, and we left him. I knew he was a very religious man, but what surprised me most was his belief that nothing hap- pens without the will of Allah. He believed in dying adhered to Allah, and if he dies on the 'right path,' he would be glad to accept his fate. We left him after our watery eyes met for the last time. We were not sure we would see him again.

Abdi and his friends at Sheik Nur Sanctuary continued to per- form the routine Islamic voluntary work, collecting the dead bodies from the streets and burying them. In the evening, they sat around a campfire, read the Koran, and prayed for themselves and the nation. I thought, at least, Abdi should be relieved to see the regime that punished him for more than 20 years go.

Abdi was a nationalist and a poet who took part in the Somali liberation struggle against the Italian colonization in South So- malia. He mobilized the masses through speeches and poems (gabay) recitation at the de-colonization rallies and gatherings of public holidays. The Italian colonial administration arrested him for his decolonization activities and inciting the people to reject the colonial rule. He received a lengthy jail sentence for his actions in the late 1950s. When the country got its in-dependence in 1960, the new Somali Government par-doned him, and he had re- warded him with a good job at the Ministry of Interior, where he worked until the military coup in October 1969. When the military took power, it accused him of anti-revolutionary activities. The Revolutionary regime discharged him from his job a few months into its rule and told Abdi not to leave the capital city Mogadishu. For the 20 years of the military-ruled, he remained 'an eternal exile' and struggled to support his family of three children and their mother.

After I left sheik Nur compound, on my way back home, I visit a vast compound near the Ministry of For-eign Affairs owned by a well-known, generous, and highly respected businessman named Mr. Mohamed Bud 'ad. He was also an honorary consul for the Netherland government. He was a relative of mine on my mother's side. Many people who came from the USC captured areas of the city crammed the compound. Some men were sitting in front of a large hut shaped office struc-ture, which was used by the owner. Many other men were chewing qad/khat in the hut, and many people, in-cluding women and children, were visible in and around two villas on the far side of the compound. The villas and their service quarters were filled with women and children.

Most of the men in the compound were former government officials who were expelled at different times for varied reasons. It was obvious from their conversation that they were longing the hour of the downfall of the regime. They were probably thinking of having another shot at a top government job, which would be a ticket to the coffers of the state.

I knew many of them, and we exchanged salaams. Most of them were from Dhulbahante and Isaq clans of the North of the country, and blinding hate for the President and the regime brought them together. Their conversation contained obscene jokes about the regime and the Revolution. When they hear a thud of an artillery shell or bomb, one of them would shout, "The Revolution is farting! When a revolution dies, it farts!" The rest of them joined them with loud laughter, which continued until another joke came along, and the laughter got louder and   rude.

The power of hate and the extent it blindfolds people surprised me. Although the men yearned for the regime collapse, they did not care what replaces it. The suffering of innocent people, the destruction of lives and livelihoods, did not sway them. They were not concerned about the plight of the thousands of innocent people and the disintegration of the nation. They behaved as though they were watching the unfolding crisis from the moon.

January 15, 1991
Mogadishu, Somalia

Remembering Vietnam

Today the rumble of the explosions from the battle areas started late in the afternoon. It was not clear why the fighting did not begin as usual early in the morning after the Morning Prayer. Whatever the reason, the delay was not because of talks between the warring sides. When the fighting resumed, it was heavy, and the explosions from the fighting areas were terrifying.

Government troops retreated from north and areas close to Villa Somalia, the seat of the President in the center of the town. The USC militia concentrated their firepower on the Villa, the commanding center of the regime, and its defenses were rein- forced with tanks and artillery. A black smoke soared from the Villa neighborhood during the day, and red flares shot into the sky at night and were visible from miles away.

According to the circulating rumors, the USC had the upper hand on all fronts in previous days, and it had inflicted heavy losses on the regime forces. In retaliation, the government forces bombarded the USC-held areas and

caused far-reaching civilians and property death and destruction.

At midday, I visited the Egyptian military attache
home. He was preparing his family to join the evacuation
of his embassy staff. He asked me to join him to the embassy, which was not far from his home. After we arrived at the embassy, we found the staff, including the
ambassador, preparing to leave the country amid the
chaos. Everyone in the embassy was either arguing or
shouting, and they acted as though they were in a burning house. The January heat added to the discomfort and
caused some of the staff to perspire and gasp for air. It
seemed that only people with military training were able
to conceal their anxiety.

The people inside the embassy compound, outside
the main building, wanting to join the evacuation
were not all Egyptians. There were other Arab nationalities, including the ambassador and staff of the Iraqi
Embassy, who were abandoned by their government.
There were also Yemenis and other people who spoke
Somali and claimed to be Arabs but were darker than
most So- malis. I did not blame them because nobody
wanted to be a So- mali nowadays.

The general dragged me into the office of the ambassador. The ambassador was sitting behind a spacious
desk and looked tired and confused. He gave nonstop
instructions to the staff around the desk, and he was
working on the convoy that was supposed to take the
embassy staff and the 'Arab' claiming guests to the airport. A plane was expected to arrive from Cairo to evac-
uate the people in the embassy. He was trying to make
sure the readiness of an adequate number of vehicles and

security personnel to take the Embassy Staff and guests to the airport and protect them from the looters lurking outside the embassy gate. A few days earlier, looters forced their way into the embassy and snatched several embassy vehicles.

The general wanted some Embassy staff to remain in Somalia to monitor the crisis on the ground. He asked me to explain to the ambassador the importance of Egyptian presence in the country in this crucial juncture of the Somalia political upheaval. Un- fortunately, the ambassador did not give us a chance to explain our opinions. It seemed he was only concerned with the evacuation of his staff from the country before it was too late. Finally, we departed, and I went back to my place, looking back at the chaotic embassy chaotic unfolding until it disappeared from my view. Later in the evening, I heard that armed looters attacked the embassy convoy near the airport but repulsed, and it arrived safely at the airport.

At the airport, a Somali mob was waiting for them to board the plane coming from Cairo to escape the upheaval in their own country greeted the convoy. The airport was still under govern- ment control, and the airplane arrived with a large and armed security team. The mob attempted to rush the airport security and the team that came from Cairo to board the plane, but they were repulsed. After a lengthy delay, and skirmishes, the airplane took off safely carrying the embassy staff and some Somali hitchhikers. The departure of the Egyptian Embassy was a bad omen. Somalis had regarded Egypt as a country that understood Somali politics better than any other country. The news of the departure of the

Egyptian Embassy shocked the people of the capital city, where violent fighting was ranging. Some of these people were even in- sanely thinking of Egyptian forces coming to Somalia to intervene and the conflict. The age-old propaganda misled the people, and the thought of Egypt being ready to assist them in the hour of need deceived the people. Egypt always used Somalis against Ethiopia to safeguard her lifeline, the waters of the river Nile. The Egyptian diplomates, including my friend, the general, always stressed the bad blood between Ethiopians and Somalis, and they emphasized the brotherly bond between Egyptians and Somalis. They even went back to the ages of Pharos when Egyptians visited Punt and other places to obtain treasures, including myrrh and frankincense. The Egyptians always wanted to main- tain a go-between role between Somalia and other countries, in particular, Somalia and Western states. Most times, that role was reserved for the state of Italy, which provided more aid to Soma- lia than Egypt. The Egyptian Embassy was one of the last embassies to leave the country. Most of the other embassies evacuated their staff earlier, and only a few diplomats remained in the country.

The American Embassy evacuated its staff early (January 5-6) in Hollywood movie style. The embassy served to counter Soviet influence during the Cold War since it was established in1956 as a consulate. In 1989, the embassy moved from dilapidated build- ing in midtown to a new compound on the outskirts of the city. The move was only a year before the country was engulfed in the civil war of 1991, and it seemed that the United States had no in- formation on the political dynamics in the country. The embassy closed on January 5, 1991, and 281 American and foreign diplomats and civilians were air-lifted by helicopters from the embassy compound to American ships in the Indian Ocean docked at the edge of Mogadishu seaport.

The helicopters came under cover of night and flooded the embassy grounds and surrounding area with blinding light. They dropped what we thought were the feared troops they call the Rangers from the helicopters. They open fire in all directions in- discriminately before the helicopters touched the ground. They quickly loaded embassy staff and nationalities and other people from foreign embassies in the country on the helicopters. Then the troops jumped on the last helicopter, and they flew out into the ocean. They continued firing in all directions until helicopters disappeared on the horizon. It seemed they did not care about their shots killing the people on the ground. It appeared the Somali blood did not matter much to them. Their operation was highly reminiscent of the American evacuation of Vietnam in 1975!

The United States had very little interest in Soma-lia after the collapse of the Soviet Union. Later, after the departure of the embassy staff, the Somali loot-ers who were waiting at gates rushed in and emptied the compound and left only the bare walls standing. They came out with cars, trucks, loaded with machin-ery, fuel, furniture, and other countless valuable stuff. Sadly, many looters were trapped in the elevators and auto-closing and dead after the electric supplying generators stopped running.

In the evening, I was told the 100-member com-

mittee the President appointed earlier to find a solution for the conflict, did not convene at the National
Assembly Hall as expected. The members were unable
to reach the meeting hall because of heavy fighting in
the area. However, many people believed the committee members stayed away from the meeting because
they feared the regime would take them hostage. They
argued the possibility of the government using them
as a bargaining chip in the event of a negotiation proposal with the opposition was raised. It was clear that
the President and his advisors compiled the committee the hastily and randomly. Some suggested that the
idea of the committee was simply a desperate scheme
to deflect the focus conflict from the regime.

In the late afternoon, in a desperate move to quell
public apprehension, the President addressed the nation
on Radio Mogadishu, asking the public to unite and for-
give each other. He warned the enemy schemes and advised the Somali people to reconcile and pray for the
nation. The people did not heed to his plea and continued to leave the city in droves. According to some re-
ports, hundreds of people were killed on both sides of
warring parts every day. The USC militia supporters
were arriving every hour from the rural areas in Banadir
and the central regions of Somalia. A noticeable SNM
help also continued to arrive from the north of the country. Sadly, most of the USC reinforcements came to loot,
and they did not care much about the conflict or the future of the nation.

Notable Isaq clan members of the Siad Bare regime
were coordinating the USC and SNM militia operations.
These SNM people supporting USC included the long-

time managing director of the Somali Petroleum Agency, Mr. Hawadle, who was the brother of the Prime Minister of Somalia, Mr. Hassan. That would have been treason in civilized societies, but in Somalia, clan loyalty preceded the allegiance to the state.

That the SNM movement entered its area in the North of the country with heavily armed militia and started a campaign of re- venge against the clans that supported the regime. In particular, the SNM militia attacked the towns and villages of Dhulbahante, Absame, Samaron, and Warsangeli tribes and many other people of minority clans. They killed hundreds of people, raped women, demolished water wells, and reservoirs and forced many people to flee from their homes. They expelled forcefully the non-Isaq population from their cities and towns to cleans the 'Isaq-land'. . I did not blame the Opposition movement, when I heard the most bizarre story of the day that stated of senior military commanders of the regime selling of arms, equipment, and ammunition to the USC militia.

January 16, 1991
Mogadishu, Somalia

Out of Mogadishu

Today the fight resumed early after the Morning Prayer. I at- tended the gathering in the mosque facing the workshop. At the end of the pray, a sheik looking man stood near the podium and faced the congregation. He raised his eyes and hands to the ceil- ing and began lamenting. He said that gangs broke into his home the previous night and threw out him and his wife and raped his two daughters the whole night. He stated that the girls continued to cry and called his name for help until the morning, and he could not help them. Even though he urged them to take the girls as their wives with his blessing, they refused and argued that they were sweeter without any commitment. He added that when he left his home, the girls were in the house held by the gangs, and their mother was sitting at the door crying for help. Finally, He asked the gathering for help to save his girls! Unfortunately, no one volunteered, and the worshipers dropped him a few shillings and left him standing there at the podium. Most of the worshippers carried rifles, presumably to protect themselves in case their prayer for protection, mercy, and forgiveness were not forthcoming from God. They exited the mosque in groups, like a militia member.

There were acute food and water shortage in the city. Even the water sellers who drove donkeys carrying water, and used to announce their presence with loud calls and tapping empty cans disappeared. Women and children carrying plastic jugs huddled together to protect themselves from the roaming gangs and criss-crossed the streets in search of water.

It became a familiar sight to encounter criminal gangs driving up and down the streets looking for people to rob or to highjack women and take them to the abandoned homes to rape. They sowed terror throughout the city, especially among women and children who had no strong-armed men to defend them. Many women and children suffered silently at the hands of these savage street gangs, and many others left the city for surrounding villages or other parts of the country.

The chaos caused by the fighting, clan-based brutality, communal violence incited by the USC, and the random cruelty committed by the roaming gangs terrorized the city. In the conflict, thousands died, many lost their rights and possessions, and many others prosper by robbing the defenseless members of society and public properties. The clan-based and unpredictable clan campaigns and the gang terror that manifested itself in the form of indiscriminate murder, rape, and robbing was one of the most devastating aspects of the conflict.

Sadly, within a few days thousand homes, all government institutions, embassies, and businesses were looted and destroyed. The gangs who were homeless and penniless before the fighting broke out, accumulated a massive amount of wealth in a short time. Their ill-gotten riches included cash, clothes, jewelry, cars, and other luxury goods. Most of them were young men who never dreamed of traveling in a car, let alone owning one. Many of them collected several vehicles, including ceremonial cars be- longing to the government, international organizations, or embassies.

In the absence of security in the city, the marauding gangs be- came masters of the streets, and they plundered the city and its citizens, including the elderly, women, and children. Many of these predators moved into the deserted and well-furnished homes with manicured gardens. They got drunk with the liquor they looted from the abandoned houses and embassies and cruised the streets with their newly acquired vehicles. They invaded and knocked down gates of private homes in search of women to rape. They snatched innocent girls and women at gunpoint, and took them to their new homes, and raped them until the victims became unconscious. Then they threw the physically and emotionally ruined girls and women in the streets.

The most affected women were from minority groups who had no armed men to protect them, and their clans were not a part of the conflict.

When the city became lawless, the minorities, such as Banadiri people and other vulnerable groups, hide their women and children in mosques and other religious places, thinking they would be safe in such holy places. They carried what cash and other valuables they could take with them. They thought they would save their women and children in these sacred places, and the looters would respect them. They put the elderly, women, and children inside these holy places, and the men sat at the door to try to stop the gangs when they come. The bandits found these hiding places, and beat the men, and raped and robbed the women inside sanctuaries. They took many women to their new homes and held there as servants and sex captives.

The country was overwhelmed by the anarchy, and no one believed it would be normal again. Ordinary people became be- wildered and could only turn their eyes to heaven and raise their hands and pray for mercy. They had lost all hope and wanted their ordeal to end. They could not endure the horror anymore and wished for a fire to rain from heaven and consume every- thing on earth. They begged God to unleash His rage and punish the wicked who caused them misery. They yearned the ground to open its belly and swallow the wicked to clean the land. They prayed the towers of power to crumble and wished the tyrants to become beggars in the streets.

The crisis continued to worsen. Many people opposed the fighting, believed it was a struggle between the regime and the opposition militias who were in search of power, and believed it would end, and they remained in their homes. However, when the conflict dragged on and turned into a clan-based struggle, and the innocent civilians were killed and abused in high numbers, they changed the mind and began to leave in search of security. Many of them arrived in the areas of the city controlled by their respective clans, and they brought with them horrifying stories. They reported killings, robbery, and rape. These guiltless and abused people included mothers and minors. As they said, most of their men of fighting age were slaughtered barbarously. Their attackers cut their throats, drove sharp objects into their eyes, ears, and anuses, and hammered nails into their skulls while they were still alive.

In many cases, the genitals of the slain men were cut and stuffed into their mouths and anuses. I was told an incident that happened in cinema Hodan, where people were hoarded and massacred. The criminals decapitated the skulls of the dead people and used it as a three-skull fire to cook their food instead   exposing themselves out to collect rocks.

The women suffered inhuman cruelty. The gang inserted torch batteries and other objects into their vaginas after they rape them. Many of these people witnessed their family members raped and tortured and forced to participate in savage acts. It was clear the warring parties, and the gangs were committing heinous crimes to exacerbate the hate and hostility between the clans. Those who aimed at capturing or holding on power did not want reconciliation and peace.

The regime was losing its hold on power and was fighting for an acceptable exit. It was like a drowning man in a rough sea try- ing to save himself by grabbing a foam. The regime attempted to implement one unrealistic act after another. The committees it had formed earlier to find a solution to the conflict were unable to find meaningful answers. Again, in haste, it appointed another committee and withheld their names from the public. The circulating rumor had it that the committee

included notable individuals from most of the major Somali clans, retired government officials, cabinet ministers, and senior military officers. The new committee was
told to meet at the National Assembly Hall on the following day. No one could explain what the President
was try- ing to accomplish.

At midday, I met men from my clan, who asked me
to join them to attend a clan meeting. The meeting was
held at the home of a prominent politician who was a father figure named Baadiye. He previously held several
important positions in both the civil- ian government of
1960-1969 and in the revolutionary govern- ment of General Mohamed Siad Barre. The regime purged from the
government pulled down him from government assign-
ments for an unexplained reason a few years back. He
moved from the center of the city to these houses in the
Booli Qaran[22] neighborhood in Medina District when the
conflict started.

I was very much interested in finding out the position of my clan future action plan. We arrived at the gate
of the house and met many others who came to attend
the meeting. Previously the entrance was guarded by
armed men, and only close family members, senior government officials, and wealthy businessmen were allowed to enter. Surprisingly, this day, the gate was wide
open for all to join. The watchmen at the entrance re-
spect- fully led us to a shaded area at the back of the
house. I noticed that even the clan beggars were welcomed and provided a space to sit or stand.

I thought the equality shown to all clan members
was a positive outcome of the conflict. In the hour of the
elite despair, all were equal. Maybe, the fairness and re-

spect shown to the men of clan this afternoon were needed not only in difficult times but in all time.

I was given a corner chair and surveyed the audience. On one side of the shade sat the government officials and supporters of the clan, which included ministers and some clan elders. A min- ister, who was the son-in-law of the President, led the group. On the other side of the shade sat the anti-government elements of the regime. They included well-known individuals who, in the past, held high offices in the government but were purged for different reasons in different times. Among them was Mr. Ahmed, a former senior officer in the state penitentiary, and who acted as the group spokesperson. The rest of the audience, which included ordinary folks of the clan, squeezed themselves wherever they found space. There were no women inside the shade, but they were observing the proceeding from the cracks of the shade, and occasionally lamented and cursed the men for not uniting and upholding the honor of the clan. The government and anti-government groups did all the talk- ing, and the rest of the audience listened and enjoyed the elite fight. A minister heading the government group first addressed the audience. He said, "I salute you in Islamic greeting, Asalamu'alaykum! I have also brought you greetings and a message from Comrade President and Ahmed." He paused for a moment and then continued, "You are aware of the ongoing attack on our blessed Revolution by the enemies to destroy the achievements of the Revolution. The enemy of the Revolution is supported by foreign reactionaries and enemies of the Somali people." The audience began to murmur in disagreement. The minister paused for a moment, then continued, "Brothers, Comrade President, and Ahmed are grateful for your past contribution, and they are sin- cerely thankful for your past support and contribution. Nevertheless, the Revolution needs your support now more than ever. We need your help to defend the gains of our Blessed Revolution at this critical juncture of our history..."

Mr. Ahmed, the self-appointed spokesperson for the anti-government group, interrupted the Minster before he finished his talk. He said, "We are not a part of your blessed Revolution any- more. It is yours and your father-in-law Revolution, and you alone must defend it! You want what remained of our youth to die for your Revolution. Have you asked yourself what the Revolution has done for our clan for the past 20-plus years it has been ruling the country, and we sacrificed our youth defending it? You said ..."

Someone shouted from the anti-government group, "Mr. Ahmed! Let the minister finish his talk!" In the heydays of the Revolution, Ahmed would have been executed for questioning the righteousness of the Revolution.

The minister continued his talk in a distressed tone," Whatever happened in the past, now we are all in the same boat! The enemy does not distinguish, and it determined to destroy all of us." The minister paused for a moment and surveyed the audience. Then, in a pleading voice, he said, "It is true that you supported the Blessed Revolution in the past, and we are thankful. But today, the Revolution still needs your support. You must see the bigger picture. I promise you the past mistakes will be corrected as soon as we emerge from the crisis."

One of the anti-government group members jumped in and said, "Let the Revolution defend itself. Let the people who milked your blessed Revolution defended it. Do you want our poor youth to die for you? Already many of our men perished for you for nothing."

Then another one asked the minister, "Did you find out now that our clan existed? We have already suffered enough, and we are not expecting worse at the hands of 'your so-called enemies of the revolution.' We sincerely believe they are our liberators, not our enemies!" The intense argument continued for more than two hours. In the end, the speakers in both groups became hostile and noisy. The meeting direction and it began to disintegrate, and it ended without consensus. When the most powerful men of the Revolution desperately begged for help from the poor ordinary citizens, it was clear the regime was no more.

When the clan officials began to hustle for help from their clans, the conflict turned into a power struggle between certain clans, and the regime and some clans became synonymous with the regime.

The USC continued purging non-Hawiye clans, which led to a power imbalance. The future of Somalia looked bleak, and the country was sliding into a bottomless pit. It was clear the damage to the Somali nation and statehood would be felt as soon as the regime with its all ills leaves the scene, and it would be difficult to recover from it.

The news coming from over the country was gloomy. After the disintegration of the national army and security forces in the regions, local militias, supported by local communities, took control of local and regional administrations. In most cases, they helped and increasingly sided with the opposition movements. The country as a whole was in deep crisis, and no one knew what was happening, including the thousands of innocent people who were either killed or displaced. The survivors lost their livelihood and became destitute, waiting for their turn to die. Sadly, the carnage continued unabated, and the hope for peace was nowhere to be found. Both diplomats and International Community representatives left the country, and the elders who were trying to mediate the warring sides were exhausted and slowly disappeared. The opposition movements of USC, SSDF, SNM, and SPM and regime-held uncompromising positions and were en- gaged in an irresponsible struggle, each aiming at ruling Somalia alone irrespective of the consequences and devastation it incurs in the process.

After more than 20 years of hard work, I lost everything I had achieved and became a foreigner in my own country, and in Mogadishu, where I met my wife, raised my family, and lost my brother and his son, uncle and niece they remained unburied. I decided to take my mother and the rest of the family and leave Mogadishu to join my children in Kismayo. I knew no one and had not visited the city before. I had no idea how I would be able to support my family and raise my children. I put my fate in God and packed the few possessions we had. I knew it would take decades, if not generations, to come back to Mogadishu.

It was not difficult to find transportation if one had

money. Looted and a few owner-operator commercial trucks, buses, and SUVs were parked in streets for rent to transport the fleeing masses out of the city. I rented a truck with other relatives to take the family out of Mogadishu. We slept early that night in anticipation of leaving at sunrise.

We were going to Kismayo, a city I had not visited before and had no relatives or friends. The distance of the town was long, unpaved and bumpy, which was terrible for my sick mother and the children. I heard there were no villages or resting places beyond the city of Barawe, which was about 232 KM from Kismayo. It took a day of driving without rest to arrive at Kismayo on a heavily loaded truck like ours.

Notes

1. A Somali folktale which states that the Somali seniors make love only on Friday nights. As a result, Somali women use numerous decoding to alert their men early Friday evenings.

2. Garbaweyne – broad shoulder. The nickname of Siad Barre's father.

3. shifta – bandit, robbers, etc.

4. Omar Samatar - one of the Somali patriots who led a militia who fought the Italian fascist army in central Somalia.

5. Somali Territories – the European colonizers partitioned the Somali inhabited territories into five parts when they conquered Africa. These five parts, which together called Great So- malia, are Somalia, Somaliland, NFD, Djibouti, and Western Somalia.

6. Mark Antony - was a Roman politician, general, and a friend of Emperor Julius Caesar. He recited a famous poem over the body of Julius Caesar after his assassination with the opening words: 'Friends, Romans, countrymen, lend me your ears; I come to bury Caesar, not to praise him...'

7. Dardaaran – One of the famous poems of Sayid Mohamed Abdulle Hasan in which he admits defeat but warns the Somali people against the schemes of the col-

onizers.

8. Botico camp – the most significant military training camp on the outskirts of Mo- Mogadishu, founded by the Italian Colonial administration. It was later named after the Somali hero Ha- lane (Mohamed Abdulle Halane) by the Somali Revolutionary regime. He was killed in the Somali-Ethiopia border conflict in 1964, while he was trying to lower the Somali flag to save it from the oncoming enemy Ethiopia troops.

9. Karl Marx:

http://www.brainyquote.com/quotes/authors/k/karl_marx.html

10. Menelik letter – See on mereja.com

11. cazzo – an I talia vulgar word

12. Medina district- also known Wadajir district

13. hakim gun -The Hakim Rifle is a gas-operated semi-auto- matic rifle. It was originally designed by Sweden and later sold to Egypt. Egypt donated the gun to Somalia after the Ethiopia in- vasion of 1964.

14. Ituri Forest people- some of the most celebrated tribal peo- ple, the so-called Pygmies.

15. Professor Goran Hyden – An Africanist and distinguished Professor of Political Science. He wrote many books on Africa, in- cluding the influential book 'Underdevelopment and an Uncap- tured Peasantry'.

16. Ainaba – A well known Artesian well in the north of Somalia.

17. Afweyne – the nickname of President Siad, which means the Big-mouthed.

18. Black Skin, White masks - a title of a well-known book written by a civil rights activist Dr. Frantz Fanon.

19. Provisional borderline - A Provisional Adminis-

trative line is an internationally unrecognized border between two countries. Examples include part of the border between Ethiopia and Soma- lia and the partition between Serbia and the disputed territory of Kosovo.

20. Hotel Taleh, July 1 Square (primo Lulio) Labor Rd, Sinai Rd- are in Hodan the Neighborhood (refer Mogadishu neighborhood map).

21. Banadiri people – The Benadiri people are the founders of Mogadishu, and many other coastal cities and villages. Some of these people trace their origin to diverse groups in the Middle East, Asia, and Europe.

22. Booli Quran - An up-scale neighborhood in Mogadishu founded after the October Revolution of 21, 1969 elite.

.

The October 21, 1969 coup leaders

1- Maj. Gen. Mohamed Siad Barre (military)

2- Maj. Gen Jama Cali Qorshel (Police)

3- Brig. Gen. Mohamed Aynanshe Guled (military)

4- Brig. Gen. Husen Kulmiye Afrah (Police)

5- Brig. Gen. Salad Gabeyre Kediye (military)

6- Brig. Gen. Mohamed Ali Samatar (military)

7-Brig. Gen. Abdala Mohamed Fadil (military)

8- Col. Ali Matan Hashi (military – air force)

9- Col. Ahmed Mohamud Adde (Police)

10- Col. Mohamud Mire Muse (police)

11- Lt. Col. Ismail Ali Abokar (military)

12- Lt. Col. Ahmed Suleyman Abdalla (military)

13- Lt. Col. Mohamed Shekh Osmaan (Police)

14- Lt. Col. Mohamed Ali Shire (military)

15- Lt. Col. Mohamud Gele Yusuf (military)

16- Lt. Col. Farah Wa'ays Dule (military)

17- Lt. Col. Ahmed Mohamud Farah (military)

18- Lt. Col. Ahmed Hasan Muse (military)

19- Maj. Abdirisaq Mohamed Abukar (police)

20- Maj. Bashir Yusuf Ilmi (police)

21- Capt. Abdulqadir Haji Mohamed (military)

22- Capt. Mohamed Umar Jees (military)

23- Capt. Osman Mohamed Jeele (military)

24- Maj. Muse Rabile God (military)

25- Capt. Abdi Warsame Isaq (military).

The map of the 18 Somali regions created by the revolutionary military government led by President Mohamed Siyad Barre, which had been in power from 1969 to 1991. The Sahil region with Berbera as its capital is not shown on this map. The revolutionary government was ousted before it produced a new regional map, including Sahil. The map was produced by UN, and it is not altered.

The Author

Mr. Yusuf Mohamed Haid was born in 1947 in Haud and Reserve Area of the Somali region of Ethiopia, which was at the time a part of the British Protectorate. He completed his primary and secondary education in Harar and Addis Ababa. He moved to Mogadishu, Somalia, in 1970. He has B.A. in History and English,

M.A. in African studies and numerous diplomas and certificates in journalism, education, development studies, and International Relations from Somali National Universities, Princeton University, University London (SOAS), University Missouri St. Louis, and Harris Stowe State University in St. Louis.

In Somalia, he worked as a teacher, curriculum developer, Managing di-rector of Radio Mogadishu, Director of Somali National Television, and Director of Planning and Training at Somali Ministry of Information. He taught African Studies at Sayid Mohamed Abdulle Hasan Academy in Mogadishu.

In the United States, he worked as a caseworker at the International Institute of Saint Louis, as a teacher and bilingual/ESL curriculum developer at Saint Louis Public Schools. He also taught Mass Media Topics at Webster University in St Louis. At present, he is retired and lives in Saint Louis and frequently visits Somalia.

www.ingramcontent.com/pod-product-compliance
Lightning Source LLC
Chambersburg PA
CBHW031203270326
41931CB00006B/385